# THE
# COURTS
## of
# Heaven

## BY
# DAVID HERZOG

THE COURTS OF HEAVEN by David Herzog
Published by David Herzog
Glory Zone Publishing

Cover design by Welly Santoso
Copyright © 2013 by David Herzog
All rights reserved.
**Visit the author's website: http://www.thegloryzone.org**
International Standard Book Number: 978-0-9911270-0-9
First edition
Printed in the United States of America

# DEDICATION

I want to dedicate this book to my
precious and awesome wife, Stephanie,
and my amazing three children,
Tiffany, Shannon, and Destiny.
Apart from Jesus, they are my inspiration
to attempt to go where no one has gone before
so as to leave them a legacy
they can follow after.

I also want to dedicate this book
to my good friend Sid Roth
who always seeks to know Yeshua (Jesus)
the Messiah in every way possible
and make Him known!

Lastly I want to dedicate this book
to Chuck Pierce as he helps many
to align themselves with the timings
and seasons of God while prophesying
into the nations.

Special thanks to Diana Richardson
for editing this book.

# CONTENTS

# CHAPTER 1

# *Heaven's* GLORY

## VISITING HEAVEN

I WAS IN BETHEL, ISRAEL, leading a tour. I had researched that Bethel is the place in the Bible that Jacob said, "How awesome is this place! This is none other than the house of God; this is *the gate of heaven*" (Genesis 28:17, emphasis added). I figured that if we soaked and prayed in a "gate of heaven" location, it would be easier to access the heavenly realm.

We drove up to the site (in a bulletproof bus, since we had to pass Ramallah to get there) but no one really knew exactly where in Bethel to go. The driver dropped us off at a spot where settlers were living near a big water tower. We walked about half a mile and found the perfect location with a big round slab of concrete and rocks all around.

I had our worship leader play on his guitar for the entire hour or so while our team lay down on the floor. Many of us even found a rock to lay our head. Then, as the music played, I just closed my eyes and let the Holy Spirit take me, as cleared my mind of any of my own thoughts. Within a few minutes my spiritual eyes opened. On one side I could see our team on the floor; but then the scene changed, and it was as if I walked through an invisible wall. Suddenly I was in heaven at the crystal sea. As I looked across the sea, there stood Jesus. I was suddenly right in front of Him. His eyes were like fire, yet at the same time pure love was pouring out of Him. He looked at me and said these words: "Thank you for touching Isaac, my people. Now would you also reach out to Ishmael?" I responded almost immediately, saying, "Yes, of course, my Lord."

Then He proceeded to ask me a second question. He asked, "Would you please also organize a conference for me in Jerusalem?" I was surprised because I did not live in Israel. I thought to myself, "Who am I to organize a conference in Jerusalem?" But, being in the amazing glory of the moment, it was almost impossible to say anything else but, "Yes, Lord," which I did.

Many of our team/tour members had similar experiences. Several of them were taken to heaven together, and Jesus instructed three people together. When a team member told me that she went to heaven with other people, I separated them and interviewed them each separately. Sure enough, they had each been together and been told that exact same things by Jesus together.

About two days after I had had the Bethel experience, we ended our stay at the Dead Sea. A fellow minister asked me if I would organize a conference in Jerusalem to reach out and bless Jewish people after they do a conference in Bethlehem to reach the Arabs and feed the poor. I told him that normally I would have said no, but because Jesus had directly asked me two days before in Bethel, I said yes. The second confirmation of my

Bethel experience was that immediately after I got home I was invited for the first time to Muslim nations to share the gospel. Within just a few weeks of Jesus asking me to reach Ishmael, I was in Kuwait seeing salvations and miracles. Then God opened up Dubai, Abu Dhabi, Qatar, Bahrain, and Indonesia, where thousands were saved, healed, and delivered.

I could have easily dismissed the experience as a vision of my own mind and thoughts, but the proof was that shortly after, that which I saw and was told started to occur.

# HOW TO ENTER
# THE HEAVENLY REALMS

The easiest way to enter heavenly realms seems to be to relax or soak to quiet music. When you relax, God can speak to you. God often speaks to His people through dreams because that is the only time they are finally knocked out and their brains are more open to receive from the Lord, as opposed to being busy all day with errands, emails, Facebook, ministry, calls, bills, etc., etc. Your mind is one of the gateways that God uses to speak to you. It only has so much memory, like a computer chip. When the chip is full of information from your daily life and stress, it's hard for God to download vision, direction, or heavenly experiences.

When John was on the island of Patmos, he had an easier time in this regard, as he was a prisoner on an island (Rev. 1:9). Or Paul, spending lots of time in jail, had the time to hear and receive from the Lord.

I usually spend the first hour praising and worshiping the Lord until His glory comes. Then I make special decrees and petitions after a time in His glory. Often, once in His presence and glory, I will put soaking music on and go further into the heavenly realm, just as we did in Bethel.

You can lie down, put on soaking music, and rest your mind and spirit, keeping your mind and spirit open for the Lord to speak to you or show you a vision or even take your spirit to heaven. Often before I sleep I tell the Lord that He is welcome to speak to me all night while I am sleeping, which results in more dreams that are prophetic or directional when I invite Him. But God will also speak uninvited in our dreams.

It should go without saying that holiness is also very key.

## LEGAL ACCESS

Believers that hold on to sin must let it go so they can easily experience the heavenly realms. If there is any sin or offense in your heart, ask God to cleanse and forgive you, and then repent of it.

> Who may ascend the mountain of the LORD? Who may stand in his holy place? The one who has clean hands and a pure heart. —PSALM 24:3

When Jesus died on the cross, He rent the veil (Matt. 27:51) and made a way for us to come boldly to His throne by the blood of the Lamb. People who try to enter the supernatural realms who are not washed in His blood and not following Jesus are actually entering illegally through a back door. Jesus said,

> Very truly I tell you Pharisees, anyone who does not enter the sheep pen by the gate, but climbs in by some other way, is a thief and a robber....I am the

gate; whoever enters through me will be saved. They will come in and go out, and find pasture. The thief comes only to steal and kill and destroy; I have come that they may have life, and have it to the full.

—JOHN 10:1, 9–10

The above passage talks about people trying to climb in "by some other way." Many are trying to enter the supernatural but they often try to get into the supernatural some other way than the legal way via a direct relationship with the Messiah, Jesus. His blood applied to our lives gives us legal access to go boldly to the throne of grace.

The Bible says to "come boldly to the throne of grace" (Heb. 4:16, NKJV). Where is His throne located? Well, for sure there is a throne in heaven. God is giving us an invite to come to heaven where His throne is. The Bible also says we are seated with Him in heavenly places or realms. It doesn't say we *will be* seated with Him in heavenly places; it says "God raised us up with Christ and *seated us* with him in the heavenly realms" (Eph. 2:6, emphasis added). That means we have a place in heaven *now*, not just when we die.

In Revelation 4:1 it says, "There before me was a door standing open in heaven. And the voice I had first heard speaking to me like a trumpet said, 'Come up here, and I will show you what must take place after this.'" John entered into the heavenly realm and was given major revelation on the end times—what is coming on the earth, how to prepare, and how it all ends. I'd say that was worth going into the heavenly realm so that the entire world of believers knows what is coming and how to prepare.

It's wonderful just being at the throne room of God, worshiping before Him. Many times when I am in a worship service or in a meeting where I am the speaker, I will lay down on the floor during part of the worship and go up to the throne and the heavenly realm. Once there, the glory will be so much thicker and often I will receive further instructions on what to say, what kind of miracles will take place, what kind of angels will be coming back down with me from heaven, etc. Then I will get up and start the meeting. The glory and angelic many times will start to break out right at the beginning with major prophetic decrees for the region, as well as miracles and healings breaking out. Often in that realm I will know where one of the big angels is standing and I will point it out to people. People will often stand in the place that I point to where the big angels are standing and will get knocked out by the power of God and come up totally healed or having had a heavenly encounter of visitation. Often when there is resistance in a certain region with strongholds or even in the room, I will go to the heavenly realm. When I come back down it clobbers the demonic forces leaving them paralyzed. Sometimes this is the best option when you sense that a breakthrough is needed. What better breakthrough than all of heaven coming down!

Once while I was in Africa doing a crusade there was lots of resistance from witchcraft. The first night was very difficult. I determined to go into an even higher glory realm and began fasting to help me get there faster. Then when I stood on the platform the next night, thousands of angels showed up and mass deliverances occurred even before the preaching. A demon-possessed women acting like a cat wanting to come up to the platform to scratch me was totally set free. Then I asked the angels to deliver the many needing deliverance, and people started to fall on the floor in droves wherever I would point to where the angels were. When they fell you could hear thousands of people getting deliverance screaming out and foaming at the mouth, etc. It was so easy, as the angels and heaven did all the work as opposed to me doing deliverance. On one night in just a short time, thousands experienced deliverance.

That is the difference between the anointing and heaven's glory. You, with your own faith and anointing, can see a few people healed and set free. But when you go up to the heavenly realm and come back down with myriads of angels and heavenly hosts, it's like the difference between a shotgun and a nuclear blast. As the days get more intense on the earth, we need to learn how to go more often into the heavenly realm and bring back greatly needed reinforcements and greater glory!

In the story about Jacob's ladder, angels were ascending and descending the staircase to heaven (Gen. 28:12). That means you also can go up and down. The difference is that when you come back down, you often can bring with you a lot more angels and a major increase in glory. This also seems to blindside the enemy and release a greater victory.

# REENTERING HEAVEN

Once you have been in heaven, either in a vision or the spirit realm, it's much easier to get back in. When you are resting in Him, just keep remembering and thinking about the last time you went up; and before you know it, you will be back in. The mind is a gateway into the spirit when you let the Lord use it. That's why we are to renew our minds (Rom. 12:2). If it gets clogged up with the cares of this life, it becomes harder.

Let's say you went to the throne of heaven the first time. Go back up to the throne again, as it will be the easiest port of entry if you were there before. But this time journey to other places in heaven, like the sea of glass. I love to just jump into the sea of glass in the spirit realm. I feel so refreshed and invigorated when I do this. Heaven is such an awesome place! And remember, we don't have to wait until we die to experience it. Many believers have their ticket to heaven but never fully enjoy it. It's like having a ticket to Disneyland and just barely walking into the entrance of the park but never going any further to enjoy the rides. Many are satisfied they have said the sinner's prayer but have not gone on to experience the joy of their salvation by fully accessing all that their salvation entails, including opening up heaven for themselves.

# CHAPTER 2

# COURTS *of* Heaven

THE COURT OF HEAVEN is an amazing place to take care of business in the heavenly place and see things change on the earth that otherwise may never have changed.

I discovered this revelation one day when I was doing a healing meeting and many were getting miracles. Then I noticed a crying women sitting next to her teenage son. I asked her what the problem was. She began to explain to me that her son was going to court and most likely jail for many years due to the police having found child porn on his computer and other things he had been involved with. The boy motioned with a guilty sad look that this was true. I brought the boy to the altar, asking him first if he wanted to be saved. He immediately said yes, and I proceeded to lead him to salvation.

Then a thought came to my mind. I thought if things are done on earth as it is in heaven (Matt. 6:10), and if God is the Judge (James 4:12), then there must be a courtroom in heaven with court cases where legal matters are dealt with. I told the boy that before he went to the earthly court, we should try to take this up with the Judge of heaven and earth in the heavenly court, which could affect the earthly court's decisions. We closed our eyes, and I told him that I could see us going up into the heavens where the throne is. Then I explained to him that I saw us going into the courts of heaven.

I proceeded to go into the courtroom. There I saw the Judge on His chair. There were witnesses and onlookers in the room as well, and Jesus was there. I began to address the Judge of heaven and earth, "Your Honor…" I explained the boy's case but added that he had just repented of all his sins and received Jesus as his Lord and Savior.

Then I felt led to ask for a moment to speak with the boy and called a time-out or a recess. During the time-out I went to the boy and asked him if he had a call upon his life. He told me that his mother had told him for years, since he was a little boy, that many had prophesied he had a call on his life. But he said that he was running from it, and this opened up his life to demonic and spiritual attacks. He told me that he was so happy being saved that he wanted to give his life to the gospel. Even if that meant being used in prison to witness to the other inmates, he was just happy to be saved.

I then proceeded to tell this to the Judge and Jesus, who is our Advocate (1 John 2:1). As we presented our case again before the Judge, I could hear the accuser of the brethren (the opposing attorney) say that the boy deserved his punishment. We countered with the argument that the blood of Jesus and repentance brings "legal" forgiveness or justification (Rom. 5:9).

Then the Judge made the final verdict. I heard Him say loud and clear, "Innocent!"

We felt such a feeling of relief. We, of course, were not sure what the actual outcome on earth would be until a few days later. During the course of the weekend, the boy kept coming to the meetings glowing in the love and forgiveness of God. Then on the Tuesday after the weekend, he went to the courthouse. The opposing lawyer and the judge asked to speak with him briefly before the case started. They both told the boy that they had so much evidence against him that it was certain he would go to jail for years. They both were Christians and basically wanted to make sure he was right with God. They asked him if he wanted to receive the Lord first. He replied by explaining what had occurred during the weekend; how he had been gloriously saved, that he was ready to go to prison, and he hoped God would use him to reach other prisoners. They were so touched by his testimony, his attitude, the acceptance of his sin and punishment, and his salvation that the judge threw the case out and he was freed to go!

Now when we say, "Let His will be done on earth as it is in heaven," it takes on a whole new meaning! You can go to the courts of heaven and take care of business. If it gets settled in heaven, things can change on the earth pretty fast and miraculously.

Job in the Bible also presented arguments for his case, pleading to go straight to the Judge of heaven and earth to plead his case: "But I desire to speak to the Almighty and to argue my case with God" (Job 13:3, emphasis added).

Job knew that true justice would only come from the true Judge of heaven and earth. Earthly judges don't always get it right, and court cases often have less than a 50/50 chance of a positive outcome no matter what the evidence. Many cases are won or lost depending on how knowledgeable and experienced the lawyer is, etc. We have the best Jewish lawyer! Jesus! And better yet His Father is the Judge. I'd say the odds are in our favor with this Judge and this Lawyer, as long as we follow the proper protocols.

It goes so far as to say that the Judge will even deliver those that are not innocent (along with the proper protocols like repentance and being covered in the blood of the Messiah). Here is a passage that shows exactly this truth: "He'll even deliver the guilty, who will be delivered through your innocence" (Job 22:30, ISV, emphasis added).

Job goes on to say, "Even though he kills me, I'll continue to hope in him. At least I'll be able to argue my case to his face!" (Job 13:15, ISV, emphasis added). Even though in this passage he was talking about if He died of God slaying him, he still could argue his case to God. You see throughout the Book of Job that he is actually already arguing his case and God is hearing him.

People sometimes ask me if they went one time to the Judge of heaven with their case, is that one time enough? I always lead them to the story of the persistent widow. She kept pleading her case with the Judge until he gave in (see Luke 18:1–8). How much more will the Judge of heaven and earth answer us? Also, there is no waiting time to get into the courtroom; the doors are always open and you don't need an appointment. Job was very persistent as he said, "I'm not letting up—I'm standing my ground. My complaint is legitimate" (Job 23:1–2, THE MESSAGE).

Job goes on to say, "If only I knew where to find God, I would go to his court. I would lay out my case and present my arguments" (Job 23:3–4, NLT, emphasis added).

The great thing is we have access to the Judge and can come to the court of heaven! Jesus' blood gives us access to the throne and heaven. In fact we are seated with Him in heavenly places (Eph. 2:6).

The accuser of the brethren is always there ready to accuse us before the Judge. All we have to do is show up covered in the blood, having already repented, and presenting our case. If the enemy tries to bring up our past or any past sins in our life that have already been repented of and forgiven, the Judge won't allow them to be used against us as evidence; they are already under the blood, paid for, repented of, and forgiven. Once you understand the protocols of the courts of heaven, get in court, and order that the enemy has to release what's held back, you can win cases and see them manifest very fast on the earth.

What I discovered is that most Christians lose battles on the earth simply by not showing up to the courts of heaven. They lose by default. This means that if they would simply show up to the court case and go through the protocol, they would have so many victories. When the enemy is accusing you to the Judge, it's time to take him to court. The Lord says, "My people are destroyed from lack of knowledge" (Hosea 4:6). We need to have not just the glory of God but also the knowledge of the glory. Knowledge of the glory can unlock it.

Just as with Job, the enemy has to get permission from God even to afflict you. Jesus told Peter that Satan had asked for permission to "sift you like wheat" (Luke 22:31, NAS). But Jesus was now at the right hand of the Father and had interceded and intervened in that legal decision and plan from the enemy to cause Peter to go the way of Judas; the enemy did not succeed. The true battle against the enemy is found in the courtroom of heaven.

The accuser of the brethren accuses God's people day and night: "Then I heard a loud voice in heaven, saying, 'Now the salvation, and the power, and the kingdom of our God and the authority of His Christ have come, for the accuser of our brethren has been thrown down, he who accuses them before our God day and night'" (Rev. 12:10, NAS).

Just like any savvy lawyer, the devil is a legalist and tries to find a loophole. The only loophole he can use is if you don't show up and plead your case or if you don't repent of anything he could use against you. You must ask God to forgive you and cleanse you with the blood of His Son Jesus before you show up in court.

One important key is to prepare your case with as much evidence as possible. You can use Scripture verses and prophetic words that God has given you. In Job 13:18 Job explains how he had prepared his case; he said, "Now that I have prepared my case, I know I'll be vindicated."

Once you win your case in the heavenly courtroom and have defeated even principalities and powers, you are given a heavenly scroll with the final verdict. Now you have true authority. As you show these papers and legal heavenly documents to the powers of darkness, they know they have no more legal authority to attack you. Also, all of heaven now will back you up and is ordered to back you up.

Another great thing is you can demand that your enemy, the thief, restore seven times more what was stolen from you (Prov. 6:31). This could be in regards to your health, finances, loved ones taken, etc.

One day when I started out in Bible school at Christ for the Nations, I took a Greyhound bus from Dallas to Chicago to meet my wife's parents, as we were soon to be married. When I arrived my bags were all missing. All my clothes that I owned, newly bought, were gone! I did not have any extra money at the time, so this was a big problem with school, preaching, traveling etc. I was very upset with the enemy. I cleansed my head of any anger or unforgiveness with the blood of Jesus. I went to the Judge and presented my case. As I finished presenting my case, I felt the peace of God. I began thanking the Judge in advance. I filed a claim with the bus company that my luggage was stolen. In a few weeks they reimbursed me with a fairly large check. After another few weeks went by, I was notified that they found my suitcases and they were sending them to me. Somehow they had been put on the wrong bus in another city. So I ended up receiving much more than justice or getting my stuff back, I got recompensed on top of that!

If someone dies and you are named in their will or a recipient of either their life insurance or settlement in a wrongful death suit, just as in an earthly court, you can go to the courts of heaven as a beneficiary of the person who was taken out by the enemy before their time.

You can even claim the blessings and even mantles of those who have gone before us who did not finish their course. Hebrews 11:13 says, "These all died in faith, not having received the things promised, but having seen them and greeted them from afar, and having acknowledged that they were strangers and exiles on the earth" (ESV).

Some did not live to see the great harvest, and we have entered their labors. Some sowed before us but we are to reap. When I was a missionary living in Europe, I would often ask God to give us not only a harvest from what we were sowing into spiritually in Europe but also from those missionaries and men and women of God that had gone before us and plowed the ground but died or left the field before they could see the fruit of their labors. I declared that we were the end-time reapers. Suddenly we started to see major revival break out. In Paris I preached for six months nonstop. It was the longest revival in fifty years in one place in France with souls saved in every meeting. Then the revival continued in large evangelistic halls and continued on when it was aired across Europe.

Hebrews 11:39–40 also explains it well; it says, "And all these, though commended through their faith, did not receive what was promised, since God has provided something better for us, that apart from us they should not be made perfect" (ESV).

God also wants us, as beneficiaries, to claim the fruit, labors, and harvest that our forefathers laid up for us but did not get to fully enjoy. He wants us to enter the harvest of all harvests in our cities and nations by asking the Judge for the release of the mantles, anointings, abilities, favor, and provision to finish the job that they started. Once you know your legal rights, you can present them and activate them. Revelation, wisdom, and knowledge of how things operate in heaven, and more specifically in the courtroom of heaven, to affect change on earth are so key.

Another time I was owed a large amount of money that I did not realize was supposed to be coming to me in a faraway nation. The Holy Spirit revealed to my wife and I that money was being held back that was ours. I questioned the businessmen if they had kept money back, and sure enough they had. They felt this substantial amount of money was theirs, since the money that we had received was sufficient, though it was only one-fourth of what we should have received. They refused to do anything at all.

The Lord pressed me to take it to the court of heaven. At first I thought to just let it go; but the Lord taught me something that day. It's one thing to forgive someone for not being honest and not telling you the whole truth keeping something back from you, but it's another thing to take your "adversary" to the courts of heaven to get him to pay back. Yes, you forgive the person or people on the earth, but spiritually you go after what was lost in the spirit realm, forcing the true spiritual enemy to release it.

So this time my wife and I fasted and prayed for twenty-four hours and together went to the courts of heaven pleading our case. We asked God to cover us in Jesus' blood and to forgive us for any anger or unforgiveness that could be in our hearts, and we fully released the people. Then we presented our case to the Judge. We heard the enemy in our minds countering with his reasoning. We countered again with the Word of God and the situation as it had occurred, covering it all in the blood. By the end of the day, we felt a total release of peace, whereas before we could sense tremendous warfare in the spirit realm. Then we just waited. Two days later the large sum of money was suddenly wired to our account, as they had held an emergency meeting and for some reason had a change of heart.

Many people go to God but don't always get results, because it is how they go to God that matters. If you need healing, you must go to God as the Healer. If you need deliverance, you go to Him as Deliverer. If you need His Father's love, you go to Him as Father. What most Christians do when they are wronged and hurt is that they go to their Father with the problem and to get healed and loved out of the wounds. That works fine for the love portion, but when it comes to justice they need to go to God as Judge. Most people never do.

Imagine if your dad is a judge by profession. You come home at night to complain to him that someone cheated you and stole your house or car and you have proof of who it is. Your dad would most likely comfort you, hold you, and give you advice. But legally, unless you go to court with your dad, there is not much he is authorized to do unless he is in his position and place as judge.

God will manifest in your life in the area that you perceive Him. If you need healing, you don't go to God as Provider but Healer. As you worship and know Him also as Judge, He can judge on your behalf. Most people think knowing Him as Judge is scary. But actually, if you come the right away, it's a great thing. Judgment day means you get what is coming to you. If you go to court and the judgment is that you were wronged and the enemy has to pay you back with recompense, then judgment day is a good day for you! That's why it's so key to first confess any known sins and repent of them and ask God to cleanse and forgive you. Once that is done, the devil has no legal right to use that sin against you in the courts of heaven because it's already been paid for and confessed by the blood. Then he has nothing on you at this point. Jesus had that advantage: "The prince of this world is coming. He has no hold over me" (John 14:30).

It is even possible to take an entire city or nation to the courts of heaven. Repent for the sins of your city and/or nation and go through the legal proceedings. The city of Nineveh was about to be judged but the entire nation repented with fasting and praying. It altered the heavenly court's decision for then the reason for the destruction was no longer a legal right that the enemy could use to force God's hand in letting an entire city be destroyed. (See Jonah 3:6–10.)

Recently my wife and I were detained in a Russian airport upon arrival for one and a half hours. They took our passports and told us to wait as they scoped through one of our suitcases filled with Christian books in both Russian and English that we were bringing to believers there. They told us we would not be able to bring them in and said it was very bad. The situation got more and more tense as higher level undercover security-type men and women came to inspect and start to read the materials shaking their heads and also searching us on their computers.

My wife reminded me that we should take our case quickly to the courts of heaven to insure that we would even get to enter Russia. As we did, within five minutes of presenting our case, a lady ran to us and said, "You can go now. Go quickly!" She handed our passports back to us. I asked her why we were detained for so long and she only told us to just go, now! I don't know if there was a spiritual or prophetic correlation, but the famous NSA leaker, Snowden, was released the same hour. We watched it on the news upon arriving at our hotel.

Even the prophet Daniel saw a major court case in process with the final verdict being the enemy of his cohorts being found guilty and sentenced. "A river of fire was flowing, coming out from before him. Thousands upon thousands attended him; ten thousand times ten thousand stood before him. The court was seated, and the books were opened" (Dan. 7:10, emphasis added).

Also, in Daniel 9 we read about the time when Daniel counted the days when Israel should be set free from their oppressors. He began to fast and pray until He had a breakthrough. The archangel Gabriel was sent to give Daniel "insight and understanding." I believe he began to plead for Israel to be set free from her oppressors using the prophetic word that he had researched that after the appointed years were up Israel would be delivered. He pleaded and his case allowed the breakthrough to occur, as he persisted until he got the breakthrough for Israel! Persistence for bigger cases is important, though many cases get immediate results.

I was in Hawaii speaking and the Lord showed me that a tsunami was coming to Hawaii and would have destroyed much of Hawaii with great loss of life. I began to pray and take it to the Judge of heaven. I sent a mass email to our intercessors to pray and fast. I had the native Hawaiian pastor and the church repent on behalf of Hawaii for certain statewide sins. We also repented for the passing of a new law that had just occurred, which was the gay marriage law allowing gay couples to legally marry in Hawaii that week. We prayed, applied the blood, and asked God to diminish or cancel the tsunami. We saw souls saved, people bound by drugs delivered, healings, and miracles.

I boarded my plane to go home. As I arrived in California on my way to Arizona, I saw the news that while I was in the air Japan had the huge tsunami preceded by earthquakes. Those same waves made there way to Máui where our meetings occurred and to other islands. The entire street I was staying at had damage and was closed, as the waves overflowed the banks causing millions of dollars of damage. But there was no loss of life. The experts were amazed that the destruction was not more widespread. Again, we were able to see destruction averted by taking it to the Judge of heaven and earth.

Moses pleaded and reasoned with God, Judge of heaven and earth, why it would not be favorable to destroy the Jewish people in the desert (Exod. 32:9–14). Had Moses not pleaded and argued his case the nation of Israel and the Jewish people would not exist today.

Abraham attempted to negotiate his case for Sodom and Gomorrah asking if there be ten righteous would He spare the city (Gen. 18:16–32). He stopped short of asking for five or three righteous people; if he had, he might have been able to win. Because the accuser knew there were not ten righteous, Abraham lost that particular case.

You can command your adversary, the demonic force or forces assigned against you in whatever way, to show up in court. Then ask God to judge the demonic power in that courtroom. If it's sickness be sure to repent and cover yourself with the blood beforehand so that the sickness as no legal right and then use Scripture verses as promised from God as your arguments in the court. Once you have finished and you sense peace, step back and rest in the trust and assurance that the Judge is now taking care of it.

I believe that we can argue our cases in a biblical way before the Judge of heaven and see disaster averted or at least greatly diminished. We can change events or the results of events by interceding our case before the Judge in the courts of heaven. Yes, we know lots of these things are prophesied to occur in the last days, but we can intercede before the courts and see many lives saved both physically and spiritually. God desires that we come before Him so that He has a legal reason to avert and save instead of allowing those to perish by default because no one would come before Him to plead their case.

The great thing is that Jesus is our Advocate or lawyer (1 John 4:1). So we have this awesome Jewish lawyer on your side! And guess what? The Judge is His Dad! Sounds like a pretty good deal to me.

Some people feel unworthy to be in the courtroom. But spending time in the courtroom draws you closer to God. Sin patterns even can start to fall off by spending time there. Joshua the high priest experienced this:

> Now Joshua was standing before the angel, clothed with filthy garments. And the angel said to those who were standing before him, "Remove the filthy garments from him." And to him he said, "Behold, I have taken away your iniquity away from you, and I will clothe you with pure vestments."
>
> ZECHARIAH 3:3–4, ESV, EMPHASIS ADDED

Right before this the accuser of the brethren gets rebuked in this courtroom type of setting (vv. 1–2).

Once you are a regular at the court, God starts to increase your authority in the court. He may even ask for your presence in the courtroom for cases that have nothing to do with you to help administer with Him in the courtroom. Joshua was invited to the court to administer and even have charge at times over certain court cases.

And the angel of the LORD solemnly assured Joshua, "Thus says the LORD of hosts: If you will walk in my ways and keep my charge, then you shall rule my house and have charge of my courts, and I will give you the right of access among those who are standing here."

—ZECHARIAH 3:6–7, ESV, EMPHASIS ADDED

# CHAPTER 3

# Angels

ANGELS ARE SO KEY to this present move of God. When you operate in heaven's glory, being aware of the angelic is so key. Most people are not aware of angels and their functions and how much they can help us. I have noticed that when you acknowledge the presence of angels, they increase; and when you release them to work on your behalf, they do amazing things. I've discovered that the more I welcome and acknowledge the presence of angels, the more powerful demonstrations of heaven begin to happen in and outside of my meetings.

Some people purposely ignore angels with the idea that they don't want to give them too much credit for fear they might give them too much praise. But often the same people will overly focus on the demonic realm, knowing the names of every demon and principality, but not have a clue about the angelic realm that can counter every demon.

For example, there are territorial angels. When you enter a region and allow the angel assigned to that territory to be released and move with you, amazing things happen in those regions. Most Christians will spend years binding up "territorial spirits" but never even bother to ask what angel is the main angel that God had assigned to that territory. Remember, the enemy is a copycat who copies God; he cannot create. He copies the structure and order of how God does things. God has archangels over regions, so the devil puts in principalities. Then there are lower level demons under the principalities, which is a copy of angels working under the archangels, and so forth.

Once you start to operate from heaven's governmental structure as opposed to starting off only binding the enemy's copy of God's structure, you can start to see some real change occur in cities and regions.

Even if you were to successfully chase out a principality without understanding the angels that are to fill that vacuum in that region, it will just come back stronger.

One day I was preaching in a crusade in Africa. The first night I had a very hard time. There simply was no breakthrough. It was an area inundated and known as a center for witchcraft and Freemasonry, and the meeting was right next to the cemetery. My host told me after the first night that even Reinhard Bonnke was very frustrated when he had come there. The next day I went into a much higher glory realm. I also praised and worshiped all day combined with fasting, and I asked hundreds of other intercessors to press in. I also asked the angels of heaven for major backup. When I showed up the next night, the atmosphere was electric. As I took the stage, I felt led to continue singing creative prophetic songs, as the worship team backed me up.

Suddenly a demonized woman that I called "cat woman" approached the stage. She was hissing like a cat and making a sign like she wanted to scratch me. Amazingly, none of the ushers would stop her. I had two options. The "knee-jerk" reaction of most believers would be to just start commanding the demon to go. That would have been fine, but I did not want the focus of the meeting to go from worshiping in the glory with thousands to focusing on a demon that wanted attention. The Lord told me I had another more powerful option. And that option was to keep worshiping and employ the help of angels. As I led the people in spontaneous worship, I could see and sense thousands of angels. The Lord told me to point out where I saw them, and I did just that. Where I would point, suddenly thousands of people would go down in the spirit and experience mass deliverances, foaming at the mouth, and screaming as demons fled in mass. The difference with option two was that I allowed the angels to assist in the deliverances as opposed to only me doing all the work one by one.

It was a glorious night as thousands were set free and many came running for salvation, even those who were far from the meeting but could hear the screams. They ran to see what was happening and ended up getting saved also. Cat women received a massive deliverance, as I simply asked the angels on my right and left to help the women. She fell out kicking and screaming, and then she was in total peace and in her right mind. We even had a resurrection that very weekend.

It went from a not so good result to above and beyond what I could ask or think simply by inviting heaven and the angelic to participate in the meeting.

Most believers' angels are so bored, possibly taking up knitting, because we never release them and work together with them to see the kingdom of God advance. Throughout the Bible angels are ever present, working with the saints to advance the kingdom of God.

First of all, Jesus gets all the glory for anything that angels do, as they are servants of God. When you see a car swerve into your lane and you cry out "Jesus" or "God, help me," and at the very last second somehow you missed the car, let me explain what happens. We ask the Father in the name of Jesus, then God uses the Holy Spirit, who is on the earth, and the Holy Spirit releases angels to actually do the job. The enemy follows, or I should say copies, heaven's ways and structure but in the demonic realm. People in satanism and witchcraft will speak in the name of lucifer or his other names, but the devil himself does not do the work but releases demons that are on the earth to afflict people, etc.

Once you know and understand how the heavenly structure operates, you can effectively operate to see changes "on earth as it is in heaven" (Matt. 6:10).

# TYPES OF ANGELS

There are amazingly different types of angels and heavenly beings. Not all are angels, as the Bible mentions both angels and heavenly hosts in the same passage but as two different things (Luke 2:13). There are living creatures, living lights, and so much more. But for simplicity in this chapter, I will refer to most of them as angels.

There are healing angels that speed up the healing power. There are angels that assist in miraculously protecting you from car accidents and injury, as I'm sure you have had some close calls that you attribute to the protection of God.

When I travel and speak, people often report seeing at least two huge angels on my right and left that many say are as big as thirty feet tall. Several seers have confirmed telling me that they can only see up to their knees most times, as they go right through the ceiling.

One time at a regional meeting in Dallas I saw the huge angel just standing there, and I asked people who were sick to stand right in the exact spot where the angel stood. Every person who walked up near the spot was struck to the floor very fast and came up totally healed. This included a man who had broken his neck in many places. He was a backslidden healing evangelist from the 1960s and '70s who gave his life back to God that night.

Another time I was in Israel in the Golan Heights near the border of Syria doing meetings. The Hebrew/Russian translator kept getting knocked out in the spirit. So they got another translator, and the second translator had the same experience. Great joy and healings occurred that night in Israel. These huge angels, whom I like to call "Mighty Ones," are like major bodyguards but seem to also assist in healing, deliverance, etc.

I can better understand after these experiences what Elisha felt when surrounded and outnumbered by the Syrian army. It was just him and his servant, who was basically freaking out thinking he was about to die. Elisha could see entire armies of angels ready to protect them. Elisha prayed that his servant's eyes would be opened to see the angelic armies and God opened his eyes (2 Kings 6:15–17). I pray also that God opens your spiritual eyes and senses to see or discern the presence of angels in your midst.

There are territorial angels. These angels are the ones that help take your city. They are the "earth or land angels." Whenever I fly back home and drive into town, every single time I am at the city limits I can feel the territorial angels welcoming me as I arrive. A wave of the presence of God bouncing off these angels enters my car and greets me. They are assigned to your territory. Life is so much easier when you work with these angels, as they can do much of the "heavy lifting."

Healing, miracle, and signs and wonders angels are also interesting. Many times when I am in very hard areas reaching unreached people groups—Muslims, Jewish people, New Age people, government officials, or others—and need God to validate the message, I ask God to release these angels; and they are more than willing. Signs and wonders, healings, and miracles will occur, validating the message of the gospel with a harvest of souls following.

Don't depend only on your personal gifts God gave you and your own faith, but tap into heaven's faith and arsenal and you will see God do things often beyond your own giftings and personal faith. Use your faith to get into the glory realm and to release angels so that much more can be accomplished.

There are angels of transportation. Several times I have been supernaturally transported from one city and even from one nation to another while driving and arriving at my destination miraculously fast. One time an eight-hour drive across France became a two-hour drive, as we started to worship and the angelic stepped in allowing us to make the meeting in time. Another time in New Zealand a one-hour drive was hampered by a flock of sheep blocking our way. When they finally passed we were so late, but we asked God for supernatural transportation and we were there somehow in fifteen minutes.

Elijah experienced these types of things and would often be transported causing others to search for him.

> As surely as the LORD your God lives, there is not a
> nation or kingdom where my master has not sent
> someone to look for you. And whenever a nation or
> kingdom claimed you were not there, he made them

swear they could not find you. But now you tell me
to go to my master and say, 'Elijah is here.' *I don't
know where the Spirit of the Lord may carry you when
I leave you.* If I go and tell Ahab and he doesn't find
you, he will kill me.

—1 KINGS 18:10–12, EMPHASIS ADDED

This was a common thing with Elijah. On the day Elijah departed into heaven they searched three days for him, which could indicate that that was how long it took to find him every time he was transported (2 Kings 2:17). Elijah's final transportation to heaven was through angelic chariot (v. 11). Angels can take you not just to heaven but back and forth on the earth. We could talk about Philip being transported (Acts 8:39) and so on.

## Angel of time

This angel can take you back and forth through time; sometimes in your sleep, prayers, or other. I know of people who had dreams about ministering in nations, such in the bush in Africa and in China. They later were invited there; so they went, taking the dream as a confirmation. When they arrived the people thanked them for coming the second time, documenting the exact day of the dream. But for the people they were really there. Since God lives outside of time and angels can go back and forth from earth to heaven and heaven to earth outside of time, as in Jacob's ladder, they can also take you there too in the spirit, a vision, or sometimes in reality.

## Angels of finances

I have had many financial miracles and seen many for other people occur in our meetings. Angels can supernaturally be released to bring finances in time of need or things that are needed on time. There is a treasurer in heaven, and angels can release things from the treasury of heaven. Often if you go to the courts of heaven over a financial loss and get the release from the Judge of heaven, then angels can legally release the miraculous provision from heavenly court cases. Or they can just supply in time. Of course, that does not negate sowing and reaping, which are all part of the provision of God. But angels can often be the messengers that bring the financial breakthrough. As you are faithful in your finances but still need the breakthrough, you can release angels to speed up the process. Often the enemy tries to block the release of provision to God's people, especially when they are using it to advance the kingdom of God, which is destroying the enemy's kingdom. Its like angels working for Brinks assigned to bring provision to you in armored vehicles so the enemy does not steal it on the way, which often occurs.

## Legions of angels

These are armies of angels similar to what Elisha had access to. We also have right to at least a legion of angels. On the cross Jesus had the option to call on legions of angels to keep Him off the cross (Matt. 26:53). Of course, He chose to stay so we could be saved. But the point is that He had access to legions of angels. Jesus said that "all the power" that He has, has been given to us (Luke 10:19). That means if He had access to legions of angels while He walked the earth and He is our example, then we also have them at our disposal. Often we perish in many areas for lack of knowledge. Once you know you have access and a right to something, you start to have faith to activate it. Once I realized the immense heavenly army I had at my disposal, I have kept my angels busy ever since. I just wish I had this revelation when I first started ministry over twenty years ago.

## Angels over creation

There are angels assigned to the oceans, mountains, deserts, etc. There are also angels over wind, rain, snow, lightning, and thunder that all come out of the treasuries of heaven.

The enemy also tries to manipulate the weather patterns that God put over creation. When that occurred with Jesus on the boat on the Galilee, He spoke with authority and commanded the wind and waves to be still (Luke 8:24). The creation obeyed Jesus over the enemy once He spoke.

When I was in Trinidad, I believe a very powerful angel was with me. Before I went I told all my intercessors to pray that God would shake the island of Trinidad for His glory, as I was instructed by the Holy Spirit. Little did I realize how literal this would be. As we arrived and walked off the plane to fill out our customs cards, suddenly a 7.2 earthquake shook the entire airport and city. It was felt as far as Jamaica. We saw the earth move like a snake and the rafters all were shaking. I discovered that the moment we set foot into Trinidad, buildings that housed financial centers involved in high-level corruption with the oil industry and the government were shaken and some destroyed. Then we held revival meetings and many were very open the message, receiving healing and salvation.

A similar incident occurred in Oklahoma City, Oklahoma, as I was speaking on earthquakes in various places. My bed shook several times such that I thought it might have been a tornado. Later I was told that up to that time earthquakes were not common in that part of Oklahoma. They were highlighting the message I was speaking.

## Planetary angels

There are angels that have been given spheres of authority over planets and galaxies. They are there to makes sure everything in outer space that God created is functioning and rotating normally. In the Book of Enoch it mentions the angel Ariel who is assigned to the planets. The Book of Enoch was at one time part of the Scriptures read by the rabbi's, and it is still a very interesting read even though it is not in the Bible we have today.

Astronauts have encountered these angelic hosts that govern outer space. Russian cosmonauts at one time encountered these angels, and it changed their life. They reported back to their superiors in the USSR (as it was called at the time), and they thought they had gone crazy since they were communists and taught to believe there is no God. All these Russian cosmonauts insisted on what they saw and heard and were put in a type of insane asylum for "retraining," as this was just too much to swallow at the time. What is amazing is that people tend to focus more on the demonic beings that also lurk and compete for spheres of authority even in outer space. That is why other astronauts have also reported demonic entities when in outer space and even on the moon, etc.

Most the world focuses on the dark side of beings in outer space but forget that they are the counterfeit. God assigned heavenly hosts to run His creation, so demons and dark entities always try to interfere. When I get the privilege of going to outer space, I will be looking for God's messengers not the devil's.

And I will also be looking for the glory of God that exists and manifests differently in outer space than it does on earth.

## Angels over government

God has opened many doors into government over the years. I received something from Ruth Heflin (a powerful prophetess) in the area of government. (She has since passed on.) Somehow doors would just open to her to speak with presidents and kings and in the Pentagon and even the Vatican. One day God revealed to me that there is a glory that God put over government. And in each glory there are angels. When the revelation hit me, within weeks I was ministering to the vice president of an African nation, prophesying to him confirming many things only he knew, as he wept and prayed with me in tears.

Then I was in the White House and the Israeli embassy in DC prophesying in and praying into the oval office and press room after decreeing the doors to open when the government glory angel came around me for about three minutes.

Another time the UN opened up. As God told me to decree, it opened when the same angelic glory hovered over me during a prayer time. Inside the UN I was speaking and prophesying about a secret meeting that was occurring simultaneously in another room to try and push a vote to divide Israel, which was stopped at the time and later confirmed.

I could go on; but the main point I want to share is that I believe there were angels of government that opened these doors. Paul was able to go to the world rulers and religious leaders of his day. He was an apostle, which is a heavenly government position. Angels helped pave the way for him to minster to the ruler of Cypress and lead him to salvation after his opposition was defeated when the sorcerer Bar-Jesus went blind (Acts 13:6–12).

Another time Paul ministered to the ruling jailer over the entire prison after an earthquake (Acts 16:23–30). Yet another time, while a prisoner, he acquired an audience with the chief of the island of Malta who received healing. Revival hit the entire island and he was actually celebrated, going from a prisoner to a leader (Acts 28:1–10).

Paul continued his journey, determined to go to Rome to speak before the emperor of the most powerful world empire at the time (Acts 25:10–12). Faith in God's ability to open these doors via angels is also key.

# CHAPTER 4

Before I formed you in the womb I knew you,
before you were born I set you apart; I appointed
you as a prophet to the nations.

—JEREMIAH 1:5

GOD DID NOT KNOW YOU JUST when you were in your mother's womb or when you were born. In Jeremiah it is written that God knew you *before* you were formed or created or even existed on the earth.

God is a Spirit (John 4:14) and He breathed "spirit" into Adam and Eve (Gen. 2:7). You also are spirit put in human body. The spirit part of you is from the eternal heavenly realm. Your spirit that God created will always exist, even though your body will fade away.

God "knew" you when you were only spirit before you were put on this earth. When it says God "knew" you, it means He had a close relationship with you. You communicated and fellowshiped with God. You and God had an understanding and an agreement about your destiny and calling.

> For those God foreknew he also predestined to be conformed to the likeness of his Son, that he might be the firstborn among many brothers and sisters. And those he predestined, he also called; those he called, he also justified; those he justified, he also glorified. —ROMANS 8:29–30

So God not only knew you, He called you and showed you His destiny when you were only a spirit before being conceived on this earth. Then when you were conceived and formed in your mother's womb, you had two destinies pulling at you. On the one hand you had the destiny that God put into you, and on the other hand you had the destiny of sin—that which all humans have been born into once we were conceived in the womb due to the fall of Adam and Eve and all your ancestors before you (Rom. 5:12).

Then one day you received Jesus as your Lord and Savior and received salvation, and your spirit began to be alive again unto God (Rom. 6:11). As you once again started to "know" God and commune with Him, you began to get hints of His destiny and calling for you. Maybe you even get prophetic words confirming things you felt deep down inside God was calling you to. Then you might even have noticed your talents and gifts that fit in with the calling of God. Finally you start to see what God had preplanned all along.

> For we are God's handiwork, created in Christ Jesus to do good works, which God prepared in advance for us to do. —EPHESIANS 2:10

God has a destiny that He has already created for you. And He is waiting for you to walk into it once you know and see what that calling is. The problem many people encounter is finding out exactly what that full calling and destiny is. There are forces at work that cloud our sight from seeing fully what that calling and destiny is. Once we see it clearly, things start to change.

We are saved and receive eternal life when we are born again. The problem is that most Christians, even though they are born again, still get pulled in two directions. When they are in the spirit, they are really after the things of God; but often other forces also pull them in other directions.

In each of our bloodlines we have relatives, parents, and (further up the chain) ancestors who had sins and also gifts and callings, which get carried down to us. Yes, you are saved; but more often than not, you realize you still have to crucify the flesh and stay in the spirit. When you are pulled in the wrong direction, often it is in directions that the enemy knows are your weaknesses due to your bloodline. It's one thing to ask God to forgive you of sin, but it's quite another to get that pattern of sin broken off you and your family line.

King David's sin with Bathsheba was forgiven (2 Sam. 11; 12:1–13), but you see the consequences of the sexual sin being carried down the bloodline in his sons. One example is Solomon, who had traits in his DNA from his father King David. There were the callings of kingship, worship, etc., but he was also pulled in the direction of lust for many women. He even went one step further to not only marry pagan women but to worship their gods, which led to his demise.

That is why often you can see people growing in the gifts and callings as they are faithful to pray and nurture the gifts; yet all the while they never deal with the sin pattern in their DNA passed down to them. Then one day they reach a very high place in God or in their ministry or business only to have a terrible fall that affects so many people. Many wonder how this could be or if they were ever really close to God. The reality is that the wheat often grows with the tares; but the tares get so big, if not cut off, that they choke out the wheat and all the good that was done. They were being pulled in both directions.

Often the success of the blessing of the increase of the gifts and callings will get people to put their guard down. They get so busy in their callings that they start to slow down their intimacy with God, which allows the sin nature to increase and take over. Many people are able to keep their sins at bay and not let them rule them or destroy them, but they never really totally allow God to destroy and kill the pattern of sin. This is often by lack of understanding of how this all works, or else they go into denial.

Paul also dealt with this as he wrote in Romans 7:15: "For what I am doing, I do not understand. For what I will to do, that I do not practice; but what I hate, that I do" (NKJV). Paul continues talking about the struggle of the two destinies in our bloodline fighting for dominance when he writes in Roman 7:20–25,

> Now if I do what I do not want to do, it is no longer I who do it, but it is sin living in me that does it. So I find this law at work: Although I want to do good, evil is right there with me. For in my inner being I delight in God's law; but I see another law at work in me, waging war against the law of my mind and making me a prisoner of the law of sin at work within me. What a wretched man I am! Who will rescue me from this body that is subject to death? Thanks be to God, who delivers me through Jesus Christ our Lord! So then, I myself in my mind am a

slave to God's law, but in my sinful nature a slave to the law of sin.

# THE BLOOD

In our blood is our DNA. Our DNA is like a scroll or a book. If you could open your book of your destiny encoded in your DNA, you could see your future callings as well as past sins of your family line; these are also encoded in your DNA. In a sense our DNA programs us towards a certain destiny. The only thing that can change the program is to cleanse and change the DNA through the blood of Jesus and allow His life to consume every part of your life.

Today scientists and doctors claim they can re-create body parts with just DNA strands because the DNA has the source code embedded in it to re-create the entire body.

Most people understand DNA to have two strands intertwined. But that is what man can see. There is an invisible third strand that surrounds our DNA called RNA. This invisible strand is the spirit part of our DNA that is connected to our physical DNA that scientists cannot see. In it is contained the spiritual blueprint of our destiny and calling. It is connected and part of the other two strands. We are both physical and spirit beings and our spirit man is interconnected to our physical and intellectual nature, and God has welded it all together.

The Bible says that in Christ Jesus we are new creatures (2 Cor. 5:17, KJV). God can reprogram and change your DNA. He does this through the perfect undefiled untainted blood of Jesus. When you partake of the blood of Jesus by faith and it comes into you, it has the power to break off every sinful pattern in your generational line. But it has to be accessed on purpose. Just having a right to it is not the same as actually activating the power of the blood of Jesus.

When you take communion you can activate the DNA of God through Jesus into your DNA. Something supernatural happens when you take the blood and body of Jesus at communion. Life is in the blood (Lev. 17:11). When you take communion you can actually reactivate the power of His blood every time you take it by faith, taking on His life which is in His blood.

> Jesus said to them, "Most assuredly, I say to you, unless you eat the flesh the Son of Man, and drink His blood, you have no life in you. Whoever eats My flesh and drinks My blood has eternal life, and I will raise him up at the last day." —John 6:53–54, NKJV

God always works by covenant. He always keeps His end of the covenant. When you take communion, which represents Jesus' blood and body, it activates the covenant thus activating the DNA of God's life into yours.

> Jesus took bread, and when he had given thanks, he broke it, and gave it to his disciples, saying, "Take and eat; this is my body." Then he took a cup, and when he had given thanks, he gave it to them, saying, "Drink from it, all of you. This is my blood of the covenant, which is poured out for many for the forgiveness of sins." —Matthew 26:26–28

The blood of His covenant seems to have been a lost message in our day. We don't hear teachings anymore on the power of the blood or songs about it as there used to be. The truth is that the devil knows all too well that when we get ahold of the revelation of the blood and how to activate the blood of Jesus into our DNA, our entire life—body, spirit, and abilities—starts to shift to a higher plane! That is why the devil uses blood sacrifice in satanic rituals and in many secret societies as it activates a demonic power. When we have the original power of God's covenant, how much less the enemy can only try to copy with a much inferior sacrifice.

We have seen people healed and delivered many times while partaking of communion, when it is done with revelation and faith as opposed to doing it just out of habit. Faith and revelation are the needed ingredients.

Since you are a son and daughter of God, you have His DNA! The more you conform to His image and allow Him to change you the more you will become like Him (Rom. 8:29). Your DNA can actually be altered when you allow the DNA of God into you. Not only will your body start to be transformed as sick cells suddenly start to be healed and regenerated, but the RNA spirit strand of your DNA starts to get reactivated and suddenly you start to tap back into your original call and destiny. Even dormant gifts, talents, and abilities can start to surface that you never even knew you had. People that were lost in drug addiction have gotten radically saved and spirit filled and changed only to later discover they had dormant business, leadership, or other skills or spiritual gifts that started to surface once they allowed the blood of Jesus to do its total work. When you allow the power of the blood to break every curse on your DNA, it starts to make room for the redemptive gifts and callings to surface once all the *weeds* are gone.

Many believers stop at salvation and never let God do the complete work of crucifying their sinful nature and desires that are programmed in our DNA. This would have activated their full destiny; they never get to see the fullness of what God has for them. That is why Paul wrote:

> Therefore, since we are surrounded by such a huge crowd of witnesses to the life of faith, let us strip off every weight that slows us down, especially the sin that so easily trips us up. And let us run with endurance the race God has set before us.
> —HEBREWS 12:1, NLT

When you allow God to totally break and crucify the sinful nature, it activates the supernatural side of our DNA. The weight that we need to lay aside and often slows us down from reaching our peak in God is the sinful nature embedded in our DNA. God wants to take you from just saved to totally transformed into His image—body, soul, and spirit—to fulfill the full destiny and calling on your life.

> The sinful nature wants to do evil, which is just the opposite of what the Spirit wants. And the Spirit gives us desires that are the opposite of what the sinful nature desires. These two forces are constantly fighting each other, so you are not free to carry out your good intentions.  —GALATIANS 5:17, NLT

When you live in the Spirit, filling your thoughts and life with the kingdom of heaven and allowing His Spirit in you dominate, it starts to weaken and destroy the desires and works of the flesh in your life. Yes, you are technically the righteousness of God in Christ Jesus (2 Cor. 5:21), but you still need to activate it. Just like you are healed by His stripes and God provided for all your needs on the cross, you need to activate it by faith to get it to manifest in your life.

Ask God not just to forgive you of sins or sinful desires that spring up, but ask Him to break them off completely through His blood, to live a crucified life, and to be continually filled with His Spirit. Then allow Him to fully activate His DNA in you!

> Therefore brothers and sisters, we have an obligation—but it is not to the flesh, to live according to it. For if you live according to the flesh, you will die; but if by the Spirit you put to death the misdeeds of the body, you will live. For those who are led by the Spirit of God are the children of God.
>
> —ROMANS 8:12–14

# RESURRECTION

Through Jesus' DNA living in you, you can activate the power of His resurrection.

> And if the Spirit of him who raised Jesus from the dead is living in you, he who raised Christ from the dead will also give life to your mortal bodies because of his Spirit who lives in you.　　—ROMANS 8:11

In His Word it is written that God can give resurrection life to our mortal bodies as well as our spirit! Imagine, every time you get sick, in your body you can activate the power that raised Christ from the dead!

One of the ways to activate this is through taking communion with revelation. When you allow the blood and body of Jesus by faith to activate His life and DNA and resurrection in you, things start to happen. In fact, it says that those who eat His flesh and drink His blood will never die.

> Yes, I am the bread of life! Your ancestors ate manna in the wilderness, but they all died. Anyone who eats the bread from heaven, however, will never die.
>
> —JOHN 6:48, NLT

Of course we know this is referring to eternal life, but in Romans 8:11 it also says we can experience the same resurrection power and life in our mortal bodies!

I believe there will be people on the earth in the last days who will literally be "un-killable" due to this revelation being activated. Some will get resurrected if they are killed. In the Book of Revelation it talks about the two witnesses being killed but then resurrecting (Rev. 11:3–12).

John was supposed to be boiled to death, and they could not kill him. So they stuck him on an island to die of starvation and thirst. That did not work either. He wrote the Book of Revelation while he was on that Isle of Patmos. He just would not die until God said it was time.[1]

Paul was stoned. Later he walked away from the stoning only to preach in the next city (Acts 14:19–20). You never hear about anyone getting up after a stoning, as it was a death sentence. You were to be *stoned to death*.

Daniel did not die in the lion's den, a death sentence he had been given (Dan. 6:16–23). Daniel's three friends were sentenced to death in the fiery furnace that burned so hot it killed the guards outside of the furnace. Yet they were untouched by the fire, as a fourth being was with them in the furnace (Dan. 3:15–27). Many believe the fourth being was an epiphany, Jesus appearing.

God can so invigorate you with His DNA and resurrection power flowing in you that you can become unstoppable to anything the enemy throws at you, unless God calls you home. Some who normally should have died may have extremely longer life spans, and others will live until the return of the Lord.

# CHAPTER 5

# QUANTUM
# *Glory*

## HOW SOUND CREATES MATTER

## SPEECH

WHAT YOU SPEAK has an amazing effect on your body and on everything you do. Speech is so powerful that it is recorded that everything was created by it. In the beginning Creator spoke, "Let there be light, and there was light" (Gen. 1:3).

Speech and sounds that you speak, though invisible to the naked eye, are real objects. If an opera singer can sing at a high pitch and break glass, then sound is a tiny *object*—like a pebble, but smaller. At high speeds or frequencies, sound can pierce through another object. Scientists call these "sound waves."

Sound waves created by speech are so small that if you were to divide the smallest particles and atoms up into some of their smallest forms inside these atoms, at its core you would find a vibrating sound wave called a quark.[1] These sound waves are embedded in everything on the earth including rocks, food, trees, and everything ever created. This means that speech was one of the first ingredients that created everything you do see and the invisible things you don't see. This also means that these sound waves can be altered and respond to other sound waves or speech.

$$E = mc^2$$

Einstein's Theory of Relativity explains it well; he was way ahead of his time. His theory in simplified terms is "E" is energy, "m" is mass or matter, and "c" is the speed of light. Basically, Einstein was concluding that energy is real and is considered matter even though it is invisible to the naked eye. You cannot see electricity itself, but you know it is real when you turn on a light and see its effect. Thoughts and speech release energy. So when you think and speak certain things, you are actually releasing matter or creating things—good or bad.

## SOUND WAVES CONTINUED

Studies have been made on water particles. Under certain studies the water particles responded to how the scientists spoke to them. In studies conducted by Japanese researcher Masaru Emoto, water particles and other subatomic particles actually responded to sound and even speech or words spoken to them.[2] If this is true, then every created thing can hear in a sense and respond in some way, as all created things were first created with the same core ingredients—sound and light. In some nations, such as Canada where it is legal, doctors use a procedure called high-intensity focused ultrasound—high-energy sound waves—to destroy cancer cells. These are sound waves. Imagine the power of speech against sickness if you use the highest power source, the Creator's power, when speaking to objects such as disease to vanish!

Start to speak the things you want to see manifest in your life. If you are going for a job interview, start to say that you are going to have great favor with everyone you meet and you will be successful. Begin telling your body that it is strong and healthy and that no sickness can survive in such a healthy vessel. Sometimes I will even say with great joy and humor that my body is so healthy that sickness does not feel comfortable around me and just has to leave. This actually works; even quantum physics, science, spiritual giants, and the ancients seem to all confirm each other.

After connecting first to the Creator's power and love, start to create your day each morning by speaking what you believe will be created—that you will be successful in all that you do, that you are full of energy, and that you will have favor with everyone you meet. This will cause things to shift from the invisible realm to the visible realm, and it will also take you from natural to supernatural health. Your health will be determined, in large part, by how well you control and bridle your speech to create health and life.

> Death and life are in the power of the tongue: and
> they that love it shall eat the fruit thereof.
> —PROVERBS 18:21, KJV

The invisible world is more real than we think. In fact, it is what determines what occurs in our visible world. Recent studies in quantum physics have discovered that subatomic particles will begin to change form simply by being observed by humans.[3] In the case of Emoto's water particles, when they were spoken to in a certain way, they would change form according to either angry words, loving words, or other words connected with a certain emotion. Everything created on this earth is made up of core subatomic particles that can be altered by human observation—amazing! Just thinking about certain things immediately causes either a positive or negative effect on your body, whether it's angry thoughts releasing poisons or happy loving thoughts releasing healing.

If this is true then objects in the invisible world change and re-create by simply being observed or even thought about. By observing something that is in your future and looking and thinking about it, invisible subatomic particles will start to shift, causing things to come your way from potential to reality. Whatever you think about and speak starts to be created.

When you get a creative idea or inspiration and start to think about it more intensely, something is already being created. Then when you start to speak and declare that you will do this or that, the reality of it starts to speed up even faster toward fulfillment. And soon after, action follows on your behalf. Before you know it, you run into someone or get a phone call that is the open door into the very thing that started as a download into your brain—a creative thought from the Creator. You become what you think and speak about.

It is even recorded in the Book of Genesis that the Creator spoke and then things were created. This makes more sense today, given the scientific language and discoveries to explain how this could be possible.

# YOUR BRAIN IS A
# RADIO TRANSMITTER

Many do not realize that the human brain acts like a radio transmitter sending out frequencies. Have you ever thought for a few days about someone you needed to call and suddenly they called you and they said they were thinking of you for the past few days? When the intensity of thought is strong enough, it sends a signal to other brains. Everything is made of atoms, protons, electrons, and frequencies, including thought and speech.

If an opera singer can sing and release invisible sounds waves at a certain pitch and break glass, so can a strong enough thought start to create subatomic particles in the form of frequencies.

I heard a story of an experiment that was made to prove that every object has a certain amount of frequency coming out of it. They took a bar of gold and aimed radio frequencies at the gold bar. When they measured the frequency on the gold bar, they discovered that the vibration and frequency of the gold changed when a radio wave or X-ray was aimed at it. Next, they experimented with a person intensely aiming his thoughts at a gold bar. What they discovered was after the thoughts were aimed at the gold bar, the vibration and frequency emitting from the gold bar was equally changed due to the strong thought frequency aimed at it sent from the brain.

Thoughts can send out a weak signal or a stronger signal. Have you ever suddenly been hit with a very heavy dark, sad feeling and wondered why, as there was no natural situation that would have caused you to feel that way? Then shortly afterwards you discovered someone was very upset with you and was not only intensely thinking thoughts about you but speaking negatively about you. Now you discovered why. Also the reverse occurs when you feel this sense of excitement like something really good is about to happen but you don't know why or what. A few days later you realize that a decision had been made on your behalf that was very favorable for you. You already received the frequency being transmitted days before the actual reality hit you.

Our brains transmit energy on different frequencies. You can transmit with as much power as you choose. When your brain transmits frequencies through your thoughts, they are picked up by other brains that have the ability to pick up such signals. What you think about also affects physical matter.

I heard a story of a doctor who mixed up the results of two different patients. One patient had full-blown cancer with an estimated three months to live. The other patient's tests showed he was cancer free. The doctor accidently switched the results.

When the man who was cancer free was told he had three months to live, immediately his brain began to send very strong signals that indeed there was a cancer. He thought about it day and night, his emotions believed it, and his actions confirmed it as he planned his funeral. Within three months he actuality developed terminal cancer and died.

The other man who actually had the cancer was mistakenly told that he did not have cancer. His brain began to send signals of healing. He started to dream again of all the things in life he wanted to accomplish. He cancelled his funeral plans and began to be thankful that he was healed and was a better person for it, thanking the Creator he was given a second chance. When he was checked again three months later, the cancer had gone into remission and he was cancer free. Both of these patient's brains released very powerful intense radio-type frequencies, which in turn created responses and signals in the body.

Just thinking about something that makes you angry, sad,

or negative can get your immune system to start shutting down, your heart to beat faster, your blood to rush to your face, and negative toxins to be released into your bloodstream. This clogs you up just from toxic thoughts of anger, resentment, bitterness, rejection, and the like. It's not that you will never experience these thoughts, but the key is how fast you dispose of them.

One rule of thumb is never go to bed in this state of mind; release it before you sleep so that it does not get into your system all through the night. The best way is to simply say out loud, "I release this situation and I release and forgive that person." Next you need to discipline your mouth not to speak about it. If you continue speaking about it, your words will re-create the situation and the thoughts will start to kick in again. Then the past is re-created all over again, along with the toxic emotions that come with it.

Another interesting concept is that if objects and people can pick up thoughts and words, imagine the power of thoughts and words if a person is in meditation or prayer and connected to the Creator. Then imagine the power of those words compared to someone not connected to a higher power. It seems throughout history that the spoken words of certain people carried much greater power than the average person, sometimes to where people were spellbound when they spoke. Some of the most famous people in history had such power when they spoke, as it was backed up by very intense thought frequencies backed up by yet a powerful spiritual force they received in personal times of reflection or meditation; sometimes in the midst of personal hard times. Many words and phrases that are used today in everyday language were once coined by such people who knew the power of thoughts and words.

Thoughts and words, if used correctly, can create situations that did not otherwise exist.

# WORDS THAT CREATE

Once your goals and destiny are observed and thought about consistently, the invisible framework starts to create circumstances for them to become reality. Now its time to kick it into turbo mode! Words that are spoken with absolute belief, faith, and certainty will start to bring unity of focus and create those very words. If, for example, you casually say, "I will become an A-list actor," but your thoughts and beliefs are not congruent with what you just said or believe, this causes imbalance and hinders its visible manifestation. Others might say, "I will lose thirty pounds by this date and be in the best shape possible and nothing will stop me!" If you speak with total conviction and passion and clearly visualize yourself thinner and healthier, then you are going to see it happen. You have incorporated all of yourself—words, thoughts, passion, and emotions—at a higher level, together in unison.

When you speak something intending for it to become reality, what percentage of power are in those words? Are your mind, body, passion, and focus 100 percent when you are speaking? Or are you speaking something with maybe only 10 percent belief, thoughts, and intensity of belief? To the degree that your mind, emotions, thoughts, will, passion, and words are all congruent with high intensity all at the same high level will determine the speed and probability of that which you are speaking to occur.

Basically, if you can unite your mind, body, will, emotions, and actions all on a high level of energy and focus, there is not much that can stop the thing you are aiming for into become reality.

# PASSION

When you are totally passionate about something that you feel or know you are supposed to do or become, things start to come your way. The level of emotion and intensity or drive is a huge determining factor in seeing it to reality. You have to want something bad enough to do something about it.

Action on your part to cooperate with your vision or destiny usually does not come without an intense internal force called passion. For some people it's getting a report from a doctor that they have cancer or some other sickness that serves as a driving force to change their lifestyle. To others it's not so much a negative that drives them, but a glimpse into the future of the joy they will feel when they are lighter, thinner, and more energetic. That joy of who they can become starts to increase their passion and drive.

You can go through all the steps mechanically and still miss the mark if there is not a sense of excitement, drive, and passion in whatever you undertake to accomplish. If you could do anything in life and money was not an object, what would you do? Start to work toward that thing in life that naturally drives you, and you will accomplish so much more than trying to do things that others expect of you, which do not necessarily motivate you. This is a huge secret to success—finding your purpose in life and helping to add passion to passion.

Everything produces itself after its own kind. Apple seeds produce apples, orange seeds produce oranges, and on and on since the beginning of time. You have natural talents and abilities that you were born with. Start to use those gifts and talents to help others, and you will have a great sense of fulfillment. This will also draw you closer to the Creator. So many people just exist and do not passionately live life to the fullest. They

**61**

have not tapped into what they are destined to do or they have not realized their natural talents, gifts, and desires. The world is waiting for their release.

# BLOCKAGES

Often times we associate a certain goal with pain and suffering. Maybe the last time you went on a diet or tried to exercise, something went wrong and you ended up gaining more weight or hurting yourself in a gym. Then a book like this comes along to really help you, but there are these mental and emotional memories of past experiences that block you from taking action. It's like your conscious mind is saying, "Yes! Wow! This is great!" But by the time you are about to take action, all these fears and blocks hinder your progress, associating this with past failure.

You have to reprogram your mind and body. You can do this by starting to associate change with pleasure, imagining how good you will feel and look, and not by what happened last time you tried something new. Also program your mind by reminding yourself of all the sicknesses you will avoid by starting on this new supernatural health lifestyle. The same is true for anything in life if you can associate it in a positive light to motivate action.

When a woman is pregnant or has had lots of pain or complications at childbirth, she may start to say and think, "This is the last time I am going to do this!" But then as time goes on and as she is enjoying her new baby, she starts to dream again of the joy and pleasure a second child would bring to her, her husband, and her first child. The pain associated with pregnancy or childbirth gets replaced by many more positive memories of the new baby as time goes on. This leads to lots of positive associations with a second child and having the faith to overcome the negative programming.

# CHAPTER 6

# SOUND *and Glory*

By faith we understand that the worlds
were framed by the word of God,
so that the things which are seen were not made of
things which are visible.
—HEBREWS 11:3, NKJV

I HAVE ALWAYS WONDERED how God could have created everything out of nothing. Although I have totally believed the creation account from my earliest youth, I never quite understood how this could be. I knew that if one day I could understand how God created something out of seemingly nothing, then we could also use the same principles to see the creative handwork of God again in our day.

It says in the above scripture that everything that was made, was made of things that are not visible. It does not say that God created everything out of nothing. It simply states what kind of things He used—invisible things. The more I meditated on this scripture, the more the entire creation account made perfect sense.

The writer of Hebrews clearly says, "Things which are seen were not made of things which are visible." So what are these invisible things that He used to create everything?

Genesis 1 gives clues: "In the beginning God created the heaven and the earth. The earth was without form, and void; and darkness was on the face of the deep. And the Spirit of God was hovering over the face of the waters" (Gen. 1:1–2, NKJV).

The first invisible thing God sent was His own Spirit or glory upon the earth. The first ingredient is the glory. Once you are in a glory zone, anything is possible. God used His own Spirit as the first major ingredient that was not visible. The next ingredient is sound: "And God said, "Let there be light," and there was light" (Gen. 1:3).

Suddenly, God Almighty the Creator spoke—BANG!— greater than a sonic boom ripping across time and space. This is the real "Big Bang" theory: God spoke and *bang!*

Only God's voice could have created everything, since nothing was created before this. So the second invisible ingredient is sound or "sound waves," as scientists call them. God spoke and everything was created. How did sound create the earth and stars and then everything else in the same manner by simply declaring them to be created? After the atmosphere of the glory and presence of God was on the earth, all God had to do was speak into His own cloud of His glory.

When you are in the glory zone and speak out what God is telling or showing you, things will start to be created at that moment. I will explain how this occurs behind the scenes. There is a difference between saying words flippantly and prophetically declaring with conviction those same words when you are in a zone or atmosphere of His glory. He is the Creator; so if you follow the same pattern of waiting for His glory to come and then speak out what He is saying, those things will follow.

The unseen or invisible *things* that God used to create are His presence and sound waves. Even God was never recorded as opening His mouth to speak anything until first He sent His own Spirit or glory to hover, creating an atmosphere conducive to creative miracles. Everything created was created using the part of God Himself, His Spirit, to create it. Without the element of God's Spirit hovering, nothing else can be created. He is the only Creator.

This is how Elijah could command rain to fall or not (1 Kings 17:1) and how Ezekiel could command dead, dry human bones to come back together (Ezek. 37:7–10). First these men of God immersed themselves in the Spirit or glory of God, and then they spoke, prophesied, or declared what God told them to speak. But what actually happens behind the scenes to cause these things to occur?

Even Einstein's theory of relativity connects to the creation story. Albert Einstein (1879–1955) was a Jewish scientist who thoroughly studied the first five books of the Bible that most Jews of his day knew well. He was fascinated by the creation account, especially as a scientist. His $E = mc^2$ theory in simplified terms is that "E" is energy and "M" is mass or substance. Basically Einstein concluded that energy is real, even though it is invisible to the naked eye. One example of energy is electricity. Though you cannot see it, you know it is real when you turn on a light or turn off the television.

Energy can also be experienced through the presence, glory, and Spirit of God. When the presence of God is felt during a time of worship, often you become energized, not just spiritually but physically as well—even though you may have been exhausted only moments earlier. Suddenly, because of His presence, you are filled with physical and spiritual energy.

**65**

The presence of God's glory releases a supernatural energy and provides the potential for miracles. Energy is substance even if your eye cannot yet see it. The presence, power, Spirit, and glory of God are not emotions that only those who are sensitive can feel. Energy is a power, a capacity for work—just like electricity and sound waves that still exist even though you can't see them.

One good example is John G. Lake, a great missionary to South Africa in the early 1900s. In his account, many people in South Africa were dying of disease. While assisting doctors during a bubonic plague outbreak, Lake was asked why he had not contracted the disease since he used no protection. He said, "It is the Spirit of life in Christ Jesus." To demonstrate, he had them take live bubonic plague germs still foaming from the lungs of a newly dead person and put them in his hands and then examined the germs under a microscope. The germs were dead![1]

The energy and presence of God was invisible to the naked eye, but magnified under the microscope's lens there proved to be a real, formidable, existing power that killed the virus. This is how John G. Lake explained why he did not get sick—he carried the cure in his body and spirit to kill disease through the power of the Spirit through Jesus.

Another amazing testimony was when John G. Lake asked doctors to bring him a man with inflammation in the bone. He asked them to take their instruments and attach it to his leg while he prayed for healing. Then he asked them what they saw taking place on their instruments. They replied that every cell was responding positively! John G. Lake replied, "That is God's divine science!"[2]

# SOUND WAVES

Some scientists (especially those who work in string theory) believe that the smallest particle is not the electron, the neutron, or the proton—it is sound, "sound waves," or vibrating strings that have "notes."[3] When you take the smallest atom known (a neutron or a proton) and split it to its smallest form, there is one more particle inside the smallest particle—a vibrating sound wave. If this is true, and if the Genesis account is true that God used His words or sound to create, then I believe that sound waves are the smallest living substance unseen by the human eye and that they are at the core of every created thing.

The Scriptures confirm stating, "The very stones will cry out" (Luke 19:40, AMP). If there are sound waves in every created thing, this would confirm the Genesis account. Sound is the main ingredient in the base composition of all created things. God spoke, and it was created. In fact, everything created was created when God spoke it all into existence. That means there are sound waves imbedded in every created thing.

Man was created from the dust. The Hebrew word for dust is *aphar*, and it does not mean dirt. It actually means the smallest created particle. I believe that the smallest particle is a sound wave, the building block and first ingredient of all things created—including man.

It is now being studied through experiments by Japanese researcher Masaru Emoto that water particles and other subatomic particles actually respond to sound and even voice recognition.[4] If this is true, then every created thing can hear in a sense and respond in some way, as all things created were first created with the same core ingredients—sound and the glory or presence of God.

In Psalm 148 God commands the sun, moon, and stars to praise Him (v. 3). He even commands mountains and hills to praise Him (v. 9). Only an intelligent God who knows His creation intimately can command seemingly inanimate objects to respond in worship to Him. In fact, all creation has the ability to hear, listen, obey, respond, and worship its Creator. Jesus commanded the fig tree to die after not producing fruit, and the tree obeyed Him. Every living thing can and does respond. Quantum physics confirms that if you study an object long enough, it will respond in a certain way because you were observing it; thus it realizes it is being observed.

NASA scientists recently discovered that sound waves of musical harmonious notes were coming from black holes (collapsed stars). Other experiments revealed similar results from rock samples taken from outer space.[5] In fact, they found that every created thing has musical sound waves imbedded in it. During the black hole study, they detected sounds emanating from the black hole.[6]

Why would musical sounds be produced from His creation? The Lord commands everything to worship Him. Hence, rock samples from distant planets emit sounds of worship that we can hear when put under special machines that track sound waves and energy.

Have you ever noticed that when you are traveling alone in the countryside, walking in the woods, or enjoying a beautiful natural setting, you often sense the presence of God? Have you noticed that at times when you are attending a church retreat camp or something similar in a natural surrounding, you seem to receive a greater touch from God? Creation emits sound waves of worship that are invisible to your natural ear, but your spirit receives them.

Jesus and Elijah often went out to the mountain (Luke 6:12;

Matt. 14:23; 1 Kings 19:11), John to the desert (Matt. 3), and Moses climbed up the mountain to get alone with God (Exod. 19). Have you noticed that you often can connect with God easier in a beautiful natural surrounding? I believe that all creation, in its natural state, is worshiping the Creator. Praise and worship brings the presence of God. There is an ongoing symphony praising Him 24/7 in nature, in His uncorrupted creation. Your spirit feels refreshed, and you often feel closer to God in nature than you do in the city where the creation is no longer in its raw, natural state.

Often we listen to music and worship tapes to help us get into the presence of God. But when you are outdoors, you sense His presence without manmade music because there is a natural ongoing orchestra of worship via the creation. Even though your natural ear cannot hear it, this invisible worship welcomes the presence of God.

When people pray against cancer, they often command cancer to go as if it is a person. Also, people pray and command their broken bones to be healed. I used to think it was strange to talk to sickness in this way. But this is possible because every created thing has sound waves and responds to sound waves spoken with the glory and Spirit of God. Just saying words or reciting Scripture is not the key. The letter of the law kills, but the Spirit gives life (2 Cor. 3:6). Get into the glory zone of His presence first, then speak forth; and the creation will respond to your word—if it is attached with the Spirit.

Even cancer responds to the sound and command of your spoken words. I believe that if you speak to the cancer while in the presence of God and in faith, believing and understanding that the cancer can hear you and respond, it will die. I have seen this occur countless times. Now, even doctors use sound waves to treat cancer. Doctors use a procedure called high-intensity focused ultrasound—high energy sound waves—to destroy cancer cells.[7] The high-intensity words you speak at the cancer cells, that can hear and respond, are much more powerful with the Holy Spirit and glory.

So if created objects can respond because they themselves have sound emanating from them, then God is showing us more of how He operated through Jesus and the prophets. When Jesus commanded the fig tree to whither, it obeyed because it was created with the capacity to hear and obey. Objects such as rocks, mountains, and trees communicate with and worship God—all of His creation not only hears and understands but also replies and worships Him. This being true, the creation also can respond to you when you speak words of faith directed by God in the glory realm.

Now you know why Jesus said we could speak to a mountain and it is possible for it to be removed (Matt. 17:20). The disciples also marveled that "even the winds and the water… obey Him" (Luke 8:25). Not just diseases but creation itself obeys. This realization opens a whole new world of authority over creation. God told Moses to speak to the rock and it would produce water (Num. 20:7–8). Satan tempted Jesus in the desert to command the stones to turn to bread (Luke 4:3-4). Satan knew it was entirely possible for Jesus to perform the miracle. But Jesus did not succumb because He was fasting and would not take orders from or be tempted by satan. Empowering Moses to turn a rock into water is not much different from Jesus' ability to turn stones into bread. Often when praying for miracles we command broken bones to reconnect. The bones can hear and respond just as all created things. Body parts and creation can hear and respond.

# GLORY INVASION MIRACLES

Why and how is this possible? In the biblical account of creation, God spoke for the first time in recorded history in Genesis 1:3: "God said, 'Let there be light,' and there was light." Accordingly everything was created with sound directing it to be a certain thing. First the Spirit began to hover over the waters (v. 2), then sound was released. So if you are in the presence of God, it is also possible to redirect an object to be another created thing. If the original raw materials that created a certain object are present (the Spirit of God, as revealed in Genesis 1:2), then sound can redirect the same created object into another form—especially if you are in the glory realm of God where the Spirit is hovering.

I believe that nothing created can be uncreated—things created only change form. Even according to the law of thermodynamics this is known to be true. For example, burned wood turns to ash but does not disappear. Although the ash seems to dissolve, it is reduced to smaller molecules that still contain imbedded sound particles. Consequently, one created object can turn into another created thing if directed by sound waves or a command under the direction of the Holy Spirit.

When Moses threw His rod down and it turned into a serpent, the Pharaoh's magicians were able to do the same thing (Exod. 7:10–12). This proves that the miracle or act of turning something into something else is not wrong or evil in and of itself. The important questions would be: Who is the source of the miracle? And, whose power is in operation? Jesus could have easily turned the stone into bread but He would not have turned the stone to bread by Satan's command because the source would have changed (Matt. 4:4). Jesus' source is only His

Father in heaven. His first miracle turned water into wine (John 2:3–9). Again we see one created form turning into another. I believe we will start to see these new types of miracles take place again in the days ahead when we will have authority over creation and have the faith and revelation to see things created change forms. This will show the magicians and sorcerers of our day who God really is.

So if we have faith to see an object turn into another object, how much easier is it to see created things multiply themselves? Everything generally produces after its own kind. The fish and the loaves easily multiplied at Jesus' command (Matt. 14:19–20). I have experienced special miracles like this. Someone planned a party for me after church one Sunday. The hostess had made exactly twenty-three sandwiches and two pitchers of water because she only invited a handful of people. For some reason, though, half the church showed up. The lady who prepared the food was shocked. God told her to quiet down and believe for a miracle. She did, and during the event she watched at least thirty to forty people eat at least two or three sandwiches each. At the end of the party, there were sandwiches left over. The two pitchers of drink should have provided enough for one serving for each person but she had enough to refill each glass— God had multiplied the drinks too!

Another time, we were holding a large evangelistic miracle crusade in a big auditorium in Paris, France. It was very expensive to rent such a place. When we counted all the offerings given by believers during the outreach, we ran short of what we needed to pay for the crusade expenses. The Lord told me to tell the counters to keep counting. As they did, the bills suddenly multiplied. I told them to keep counting until they came to a certain amount that was enough to cover all the expenses. We ended up with above and beyond what we needed, as God had supernaturally multiplied the finances. We have seen this miracle many times over.

We are also witnessing many people receive instant weight loss during our meetings. One man in Tennessee lost seventy pounds in one service after receiving a word of knowledge. In Las Vegas during the first night of meetings, about twenty women lost weight equal to five dress sizes. God can just as easily remove fat cells as we can put them on. As you start to meditate on this revelation and on how big God really is, you will begin to believe; and then you will see these same miracles happen in your own life.

We have witnessed many financial miracles and debt cancellation in our meetings as well. After people have given to the work of God, because of the creative miracle realm, they notice extremely fast money miracles. Some even find money in their pockets and purses immediately after placing an offering in the basket. Others have discovered thousands of dollars in their bank account that were not there before. God performed the same miracles: multiplying resources for the widow, feeding the crowd with loaves and fish, prospering Peter with many fish, placing the gold coin in a fish's mouth to pay the taxes, and many more examples of God's glorious provision miracles. (See 1 Kings 7:10–16; John 6:11; Matthew 14:19–20; 15:36–37; Mark 8:6–8; John 21:3–11; Matthew 17:24–27.)

In our meetings we are seeing more and more bald people receive instant hair growth. A lady in Prescott, Arizona, received hair growth while we were all watching! We actually saw her bald spots filling in with hair. In Augusta, Georgia, hair appeared instantly on top of a man's head where he was totally bald and the color of his hair was its original dark color. We have also seen people with white hair have their hair returned to its original hair color. It is amazing to watch these transformations.

So, if everything created cannot be destroyed but is only converted into another form, then the hair still exists somewhere—it has just been converted to another form, but it still exists. There is no distance in the glory; so wherever your hair is, it can still respond. And because your hair has sound waves and can hear and respond, when I am in the glory zone in a meeting, I can call out, "Hair, come back." It can return to its original state and respond to my words spoken under the direction of the Holy Spirit. God cares about every hair on your head (Matt. 10:30; Luke 12:7); how much more He cares for the pressing needs and problems in your life.

How do you think Ezekiel was able to prophesy and speak to bones and say, "Dry bones, hear the Word of the LORD!" (Ezek. 37:4)? God was telling him to speak to bones—not demons, people, God, or angels; but bones! And when he did, they responded as proof that they could hear and obey. Then even the sinews and flesh joined in and reformed. How could the flesh that was dissolved return? Again, nothing created is really gone, it only changes form into smaller molecules and atoms we cannot see. At the sound of God's command, they are reformed. Ezekiel even prophesied over the dry bone's breath, which is their spirit when translated from the original, and it also obeyed and returned. (See Ezekiel 37:5–10.) How would the bones know which bones to reconnect to after so many years? Apparently created things have a memory just as we have a memory.

At a health clinic in Mexico, an organic garden field was cultivated and maintained normally; with the exception that the owner told the gardeners to show lots of love, care, and attention to the plants growing only in half of the garden. At the end of the growing season, the half of the garden that was treated kindly produced twice as much crop as the other half.

In another experiment at the same clinic, a man had two trees growing in front of his window. He projected hate and anger toward one tree and to the other he expressed love. In six weeks the tree that received hate and anger withered and almost died, the other tree flourished. Creation responds to what humans say and do.[8]

The Bible says the earth swallowed up Korah and his rebellion (Num. 16:32). It is possible that the earth where he was standing got tired of his sin and rebellion. I believe that there are geographical locations on the earth where sin has reached such a high level that the earth, waves, and the elements have turned against man, as they can no longer tolerate the enormity of filth. This will become more and more evident in the last days as sin abounds in certain cities more than others, and where there is not enough light to counteract the darkness. The Bible even says that the creation itself groans with birth pangs for the manifestation of the sons and daughters of God (Rom. 8:19–22).

# IF WALLS COULD TALK

I led a tour to Israel recently, and our friend and missionary pastor was with us. He had been struggling for eight years with the idea that Israel had a special place in God's heart. He grew up on replacement theology. No matter what Scriptures he read that showed him how God was still dealing with the Jewish people, he could not get the revelation. But he did see the effects and blessings of those who pray and love Israel and the Jewish people. He decided to go to Israel for understanding and insight.

The first day we visited the Western Wall in Jerusalem. The pastor leaned his head against the wall and prayed. Within minutes he broke out in great tears and weeping. This was very unusual for him, as his personality was more reserved and analytical, especially concerning Israel. After the incident he told me that somehow at the wall he suddenly understood the last 3,000 years of Jewish history and began to accept Israel's place in the end times. I was surprised that he so quickly changed his mind after leaning against the wall for only a few minutes; after all, I had been explaining the subject to him for eight years.

But the wall offered thousands of years of witness to things that occurred, including Jesus' teachings and healings, the temple cleansing, the Last Supper with the disciples, the persecution, and the empty tomb. They had been there all along, and the sound waves were still emanating from the rock wall—not only worshiping, but explaining the true story of God's covenant people and why they are here today. The walls spoke to his spirit and downloaded 3,000 years of history and revelation to him. Again, if created objects can emit sounds waves of worship to God who is a Spirit, then it is also possible for our spirit to pick up those same sound waves still resonating off of created objects and also know things from the past that bring revelation.

Recently after sharing this revelation, the following story was told to me. A little girl was having nightmares while sleeping in her bedroom. The family had just moved into the house; the girl never had nightmares before. She was able to sleep peacefully in other rooms but not in her room. Even after the family prayed several times about it, in her bedroom she kept having the same dream about a murder and how it happened. Finally, after praying, the parents decided to call the former homeowners and find out if there was anything unusual that occurred in that room. They were told that a murder actually took place in that room, and it happened exactly as the girl had seen it in her dream. The walls witnessed the murder and retold the story to the little girl in her dreams. The family prayed over the walls commanding not only the spirit of murder to leave, but also the memory of what happened there to be washed away by the blood of Jesus.

The blood of the sin of murder was crying out in that situation. The Bible mentions the blood of the martyrs crying out. The actual blood of the martyrs speaks; not just the martyrs, but also their blood. Again we realize that all things have a voice, and sound can be carried over time to be experienced again.

Just as an object can carry on it the weight and presence of God—as Paul's handkerchief, Samson's jawbone of a donkey, and Moses' rod—they can also carry memories of the past and both good and evil things that are part of it (Acts 19:11; Judg. 15:15; Exod. 4:2–5). After Elisha died, his bones still had the power, glory, and sound of God emanating from them. A dead man was thrown over Elisha's bones in a grave and the dead man was resurrected as the glory still resided there, possibly many years later (2 Kings 13:21).

We have prayed over objects and saturated them with the power of God. During a crusade I was conducting, two crippled people got up and walked after a simple word from God. Another crippled man left the meeting early. His wife drove him to the hotel. As she was picking up the keys inside the hotel, a man stole the car with the crippled man in it. The thief pushed the man out of the moving car and the seat belt caught around his leg, tearing it from his body. He was found bleeding by the side of the road. The ambulance took him to the hospital emergency room and the doctors grafted the torn and already paralyzed leg back onto his body.

During the meeting that night after we saw the two crippled people walk, we prayed over tissue boxes and saturated them with the same glory that was in the room causing the other miracles. People sent tissues to friends who were healed after receiving them. One woman took a tissue to the man in the hospital and placed it on his mangled leg that the doctors had tried to regraft to his body. Suddenly he began to feel electricity run down his leg—totally amazing since he was paralyzed and his leg had just been reattached after being traumatically torn off. Soon he was wiggling his toes; another miracle. By the fifth day he was released from the hospital and able to walk! Although his leg had been dead weight from being crippled and then the subsequent trauma of being torn off, he could walk. God is amazing!

That is an awesome true story, but how did it happen? Well, if energy is equal to matter or mass, then that means the glory of God—which is supernatural power and energy—is also matter and has weight. Though you can't see it, His glory has weight and matter and actually exists. When you saturate a tissue with the glory—the substance and weight of God—it will be heavier than before it was saturated; it has weight that it did not have before. The object simply holds and transfers that same glory and then releases it when placed on someone by faith.

The glory can also be carried by invisible sound waves traveling through time and space. For example, when you watch a miracle crusade on television that was filmed three months previously and you get healed while watching it and feel the awesome presence of God, the glory has traveled through time and space to you. Even though you were not there when the actual crusade took place, whenever you watch it the same glory is reactivated and you receive the same impartation, healing, or blessing as if you were there three months ago. The glory of the meeting that took place at a particular time is frozen when taped and then unfrozen and reactivated the moment you watch it. So the voice waves of the one speaking, the worship, and the very atmosphere in that meeting can be contained in sound and light in the form of images and can be reactivated.

I once experimented with this belief. I was watching some never-before-seen footage of one of A. A. Allen's ministry meetings. Although the meeting was taped fifty years previously, I could sense the same glory, power, and excitement in his voice—it seemed as if I was there. It was not just an emotional feeling because I also felt the same glory. I watched as he pulled paralyzed people up out of wheelchairs. That night I was to preach in a revival meeting. A crippled woman came up to me; and almost without thinking and full of faith, I told her to stand up and walk. I took her hand and helped her up, and she walked for the first time! There was an impartation from a revival from the 1950s frozen in time that was waiting for me to release it and receive it by pushing the play button on the VCR.

# CHAPTER 7

# SYNCING
## with *Heaven*

WHEN YOU SYNC WITH HEAVEN, things happen on earth as it is in heaven. One of the ways to be in sync with heaven is to do things when heaven does them.

One of the ways is to worship God at His "appointed times." Everyday we should spend time with God, but there are certain times a year God asks us to set aside time with Him and He promises "special" blessings that would not come any other way. These appointed times are the feasts of God. The three major ones are Passover, Pentecost, and the Fall Feasts leading into the Feast of Tabernacles.

When you celebrate these feasts at the appointed times that God set up, you see amazing heavenly abundance in multiple ways. Imagine if after Jesus' death they stopped celebrating Pentecost and never met in that Upper Room yet one more time. That year, right after Jesus had been crucified and resurrected, the Holy Spirit showed up and filled everyone with the baptism of the Holy Spirit.

You see, in heaven there are things that occur at appointed times. Heaven is the realm of eternity. God mentioned that these feasts were to be celebrated eternally. When you tap into the exact timing of what is occurring in heaven, a major heavenly download occurs, which I like to call seasonal portals.

Many people have heard about geographical portals or places where God's glory and presence reside, but there are also "seasonal" portals or appointed times that the Bible clearly says that God has set on the calendar waiting for us to meet with Him in a special way. It's like a birthday. You love your spouse or child every day, but once a year there is a special celebration of that loved one. Let's focus on the three major appointed times.

# PASSOVER

For years, without ever having any revelation on the feasts, I have always noticed the glory, power, blessing, and harvest of souls to be greater when I am doing meetings during these times than at other times. Now we purposefully do many of our conferences and outreaches during these times, and we always see "over the top" levels of God's glory, miracles, signs and wonders, salvations, revelation, and provision.

We started our Paris in the Glory Crusades in Paris, France, during Passover of 2001. God blessed each conference after that so much that we began holding a crusade every three months in a large arena that Benny Hinn and Morris Cerullo would rent when they came to that nation. We would see Muslims, Jews, Europeans, and others who otherwise would never be so open, run to be saved. There always seemed to be an unusual grace for this sudden, unexpected openness to the gospel. The meetings, along with the miracles, signs, and creative miracles, were so amazing that most people only hear about them in third world countries.

We continue to do these meetings in Sedona, Arizona, and all over the U.S., with the greatest open heaven and glory encounters that many who have come can attest to. At our last conference in Sedona during Passover, people flew in from the four corners of the U.S., the Caribbean, Italy, Austria, and Hungary, and experienced creative miracles, the manifestation of the fragrance of the Lord, and other miracles.

In June 2008 in Sedona, Arizona, during the Feast of Pentecost, we held our Pentecost Glory Conference. The seasonal portal opened up and suddenly angels were audibly heard singing and sounds were coming from the atmosphere that caused the waiters and workers in the resort to run into our meetings asking where those sounds were coming from. It was the most glorious presence we ever had, and each series of meetings gets better than the last.

Steve Swanson, who was leading worship one day, began to weep as he testified that he was not touching any of the instruments or keyboards. Everyone saw him shaking his head as the angels began singing during the message. Also, we saw miracles such as thyroid problems and cancers heal, deaf ears open, instant weight loss miracles, cataracts disappear, and many other signs and wonders too numerous to list here. During one of the meetings, the Lord told us not to take an offering because all the expenses would be taken care of. A few minutes later, as I was leaving the meeting, a businessman came up and told us God asked him to pay all the expenses of the conference, which he did. Everything seems to flow effortlessly when we hit the seasonal portal.

Jesus' Last Supper with His disciples was none other than

the Passover meal during the Feast of Passover. If even Jesus and the apostles celebrated Passover, then to Jesus it must be important.

In fact, Jesus renewed the covenant of blood sacrifice with us to reopen the ancient pathway with His own blood. That is why both Jewish and Gentile believers continued to celebrate Passover for many years after His death—it was not only connected with Israel escaping from Egypt but with Jesus becoming our Passover Lamb.

We see this begin to change hundreds of years later after Jerusalem had already been destroyed by the Romans due to a Jewish Rebellion in AD 66 (which is well documented in world history books) that led to its destruction by AD 70. Jesus prophesied this would occur in Matthew 24:2.

Due to this, by AD 325, during the time of Constantine, there still was much anti-Israel sentiment as Rome was now the new headquarters of much of the church for both Jewish and Gentile believers. Constantine began to close up this ancient pathway by abolishing the celebration of Passover and other biblical feasts at the biblical times and replacing them with other hybrid forms. For instance, Passover became a mixture of Jesus' death and resurrection and a pagan celebration—celebrated on a different day and with a different name. Constantine called it Easter, after Ishtar, who was the goddess of fertility and whom many in pagan Rome still worshiped.

By doing this Constantine thought he could please the many new believers in Jesus but still mix in pagan practices on pagan holidays to also please the pagans. Traditions like Easter egg hunts originated from such pagan practices. "There is no indication of the observance of the Easter festival in the New Testament, or in the writings of the apostolic Fathers....The first Christians [the original true church]...continued to observe the

Jewish [that is, God's] festivals, though in a new spirit, as commemorations of events which those festivals had foreshadowed. Thus the Passover, with a new conception added to it, of Christ, as the true Paschal Lamb and the first fruits from the dead, continued to be observed."[1]

How could the church have moved in such power and unity at its inception in Israel, spread all over the Roman Empire with miracles and resurrections, and yet eventually be degraded to a form of religion denying the power?

The feasts are not so much rules today to attain any sense of holiness as they are God's perspective and revelation from heaven so that things on earth may be aligned with what goes on in heaven. God promised to visit His people during specific seasons of time known as the feasts. And if God opened the heavens in both the Old and New Testament during these seasons, like during the Feast of Pentecost where an entire new glory in the church and the baptism of the Holy Spirit was ushered in, why would the same God of yesterday, today, and forever (Heb 11:13) not show up in the same and even greater extraordinary ways again today during these seasons—these divine appointments with God when we purposefully take the time out to worship Him and feast on Him? The fact that God even restores, for example, the Feast of Tabernacles (see Zechariah 14 about its restoration in the last days upon His return to earth with the Messiah now as the reason for the season) points to the fact that these are seasons in God where we can expect God to visit us according to His Word. Jesus even told them to wait for the promises to be fulfilled after His departure in certain kairos seasons of time (Luke 24:49; Acts 1:4).

# PENTECOST

When the early church obeyed Jesus' command to wait in the Upper Room, many do not realize that they waited in the Upper Room during the Feast of Weeks (or Pentecost), a feast that had been celebrated by Israel for centuries. (See Exodus 34:21–23; Leviticus 23:15–22; Deuteronomy 16:9–12, 16; 2 Chronicles 8:13; Ezekiel 1:13.) This was one of the feasts that God told Moses and the Israelites to celebrate. For Israel, the Feast of Weeks is all about celebrating the giving of the Law and the Ten Commandments.

This is part of reactivating the mantle that Moses walked in; but now it is for all believers. When the disciples obeyed and waited on the Lord during that specific feast, praising and worshiping Him, the heavens opened and the power of God was released. All believers went out from there full of the Holy Spirit, doing healings, miracles, signs, and deliverances, as boldness came upon them.

This power at Pentecost was not released in the years before because they did not yet have access into the supernatural that came through the blood sacrifice. The blood of Jesus became the first doorway into the supernatural; now all believers could experience the supernatural as Moses once had. Now believers moved powerfully in both the Word and the Spirit.

By the way, when Peter preached that day, he did not quote from the New Testament or the Book of Acts, for they had not yet been written. He and all the believers read from the ancient Hebrew Scriptures, now often referred to as the Old Testament. When they reread and preached these scriptures with revelation, as the blood of Jesus provided access to the supernatural, the same power and glory that Moses and Elijah experienced was released.

# TABERNACLES

The Feast of Tabernacles is also a very powerful seasonal portal that many are starting to realize once again. It is so powerful that when Messiah the King returns to rule and reign in Jerusalem, Zechariah 14:16 says He will restore this feast. This is another ancient pathway to the glory of God.

> And it shall come to pass that everyone who is left
> of all the nations which came against Jerusalem shall
> go up from year to year to worship the King, the
> LORD of hosts, and to keep the Feast of Tabernacles.
> —ZECHARIAH 14:16, NKJV

Israelites celebrated this feast, as did the early church (including Gentile believers), for the first few hundred years. If Jesus is going to restore the feasts that have been forgotten, including the Feast of Tabernacles, why not tap into this seasonal portal and the future blessings it releases now? Many think it is only a Jewish feast; but, according Zechariah, it is a feast for all nations.

> And it shall be that whichever of the families of the
> earth do not come up to Jerusalem to worship the
> King, the LORD of hosts, on them there will be no
> rain.                           —ZECHARIAH 14:17, NKJV

God is promising to open the heavens and pour out rain if we will simply honor Him during this exact time. How each person, group, or church celebrates Him is really not the point, but taking the time to honor God during Tabernacles is a major key. Rain is symbolic of both spiritual and material blessings.

God will open the heavens and pour out rain on people and nations who will walk into this seasonal portal both now and in the future. This feast is a major seasonal portal, and Jerusalem itself is a physical portal. When you combine a geographical portal with a seasonal portal (as will occur when the King returns to Jerusalem), the result is heaven on earth. Though to many it may now appear optional to celebrate these feasts—as our salvation is not dependent on these ancient pathways or feasts but on the sacrifice Jesus paid on the cross, it does allow us to tap into a greater glory. And we now know that it will be mandatory if we want His "rain" at His return (see Zech. 14:17–18).

God is so serious about His invitation that when the King returns, serious consequences will occur for those who choose not to respond to His invitation to the holy party.

> If the family of Egypt will not come up and enter in,
> they shall have no rain; they shall receive the plague
> with which the LORD strikes the nations who do not
> come up to keep the Feast of Tabernacles.
> —ZECHARIAH 14:18, NKJV

Even Arab nations will be not only invited but required to enter into this time of open heaven encounters during the feast in Jerusalem. In fact, Zechariah lists plagues that will come if these nations choose to pass on the invitation. This again proves that the feast is not a Jewish feast but a feast for all nations who will worship Jesus, the Jewish Messiah, as the King of the earth. The other side to this is the physical portal. When the Gentile nations come to Jerusalem, they are admitting that God has chosen Jerusalem and Israel as the biggest portal on the earth for His glory.

I believe that when Arab believers begin to celebrate Jesus purposely during these seasonal portals—even in their own nations right now—great "rain," revival, and harvest will erupt like never before in the Arab nations and all nations of the world.

God will also use the Arab believers to make the Jews jealous for their Messiah, for they will see Arab believers rejoicing before God and God manifesting His power and glory among them. The Jews will wonder why God is showing up among the Gentiles. They will find their answer in the access all believers have been granted through the blood sacrifice of Jesus.

# SHABBAT

> There remaineth therefore a rest to the people of God. For he that is entered into his rest, he also hath ceased from his own works, as God did from his. Let us labour therefore to enter into that rest, lest any man fall after the same example of unbelief.
>
> —HEBREWS 4:9–12, KJV

A weekly heavenly seasonal portal can occur also. God designed humans to rest once a week. It is even written in the Ten Commandments. When you take one day a week to rest from your usual income-earning labors and spend time with God, read His Word, enjoy His creation, and spend quality time with family, you tap into a supernatural dimension of rest you would not otherwise have experienced. Biblical Shabbat, observed from Friday night sundown until Saturday night sundown, is practiced even today in Israel and in Jewish families around the world. Christians often take Sunday off. But I've noticed that rushing to church sometimes twice that day is not always a rest. I still enjoy taking my Friday night to Saturday off. It makes a huge difference in my week. Often I am speaking on the weekends, so I will do a Friday night service then sleep in and enjoy deep rest and intimacy with the Lord, often going for a walk in nature. As I do, fresh creative ideas from heaven will just flow.

When I don't get that one day off, I can feel a huge difference. When I rest that day I am more clear minded and my body is relaxed; I feel happier. I am able to put all the business of life on pause, redirect my life, and reevaluate my destiny to make sure it's on the right track. Often I get fresh direction and visions that day.

Busyness and stress can abort your destiny. I literally can't wait every week for Shabbat. It's not a burden at all but a blissful rest basking in the stress-free glory and presence of God. It's a taste of heaven on earth. I look forward to my weekly twenty-four hour date with Jesus!

## FIRST FRUITS—ROSH CHODESH

Like Shabbat is weekly, First Fruits is a monthly pause to seek the Lord, worship together with His people, receive from the prophetic, and give to God. What we do during that first day of the month will determine the blessing of the next thirty days. You are in essence giving God the first fruit or the first day of that month, asking Him to bless the rest. Once I tapped into this revelation, the favor and breakthroughs have been mind-boggling. I really think the enemy has kept away much of the needed revelation in the Word of God to keep us from reaching our highest potential in God and in life in general. He tries to make us think that these things are no longer for us today, when actually we are invited to the same blessings of Abraham as the Jews have as we are grafted in through Jesus our Jewish Messiah. We are the adopted kids; we get to show up to the celebrations too!

This monthly cycle falls on the new moon of each month. A good Hebrew calendar will help you know what day is the first day of first fruits each month from sundown to sundown. (See Numbers 28:11–15; Psalm 81:3–4; 1 Samuel 20: 5, 18; 2 Kings 4:23; Isaiah 66:23.)

I also recommend a great book on this subject, *A Time to Advance,* by Chuck Pierce with Robert and Linda Heidler.

# CHAPTER 8

# VIBRATIONAL
# *Glory*

In the beginning God (prepared, formed, fashioned,
and) created the heavens and the earth. The earth
was without form and an empty waste, and darkness
was upon the face of the very great deep. The Spirit
of God was moving (hovering, brooding) over the
face of the waters.                —GENESIS 1:1–2, AMP

WHEN THE GLORY of God is vibrating (or brooding) at a high
frequency, it propels you to levels of power and glory that literally
effect change on the earth, whether it is cancer, supernatural transportation, miracles, victory, favor, or anything else God is doing.

The higher you are vibrating in God's glory the better.
Moses was in such a level of glory that the people could not
even look upon His face (Exod. 34:29–35; 2 Cor. 3:7–18). The
light of the glory of God shone through him as he became
translucent, beaming light through his skin. Jesus, just after His
resurrection, was in such a level that His human body could lit-

erally go through the walls (John 20:26), or He could walk on water after having spent all night in prayer (Matt. 14:23–25).

There are things you can do to increase your vibrational frequency of the Holy Spirit moving through you at super high speed, obliterating obstacles, setting people free, healing them, and producing speedy results from the power of your words in prayer. Let's start with some practical things you can do to increase your vibrational frequency of God's glory.

**Praise and worship**

When you praise and worship God, it electrifies the atmosphere and literally acts like a magnet attracting God's glory, the angelic, and His sweet presence.

Paul and Silas were constrained by their physical surroundings, being in chains in a high security prison. They began to praise and worship, and the earth began to move along with the worship as an earthquake erupted destroying the prison and setting them free along with the salvation of the other prisoners and the jailer (Acts 16:23–34). Praise and worship causes you to vibrate at a very high frequency because your entire being is in the spirit realm. Not just your mind and voice, but even your body starts to feel different and even more supernatural as the cells in your body start to worship as well. King David said, "My soul yearns, yes, even pines and is homesick for the courts of the Lord; my heart and my flesh cry out and sing for joy to the living God" (Ps. 84:2, AMP).

**Holiness**

When you are living in God's standard of holiness, it increases the glory of God. Sin weakens and lowers your vibrational frequency while holiness increases it. Sin causes the glory of God to leak out of our beings, while holiness helps us to contain the glory that God is pouring out during prayers and worship. Repentance is the most powerful way to get back into God's glory and intimacy which increases the vibration of God's glory over your life (Isa. 57:15).

## Fasting

Fasting is super powerful and one of the least used options in the Western world. All through the Bible we see fasting resulting in major supernatuaral revelation, angelic visitation, breakthrough, revival, ovecoming attacks and temptation, and direction. Even Jesus fasted; and after He did, it is recorded that He came out of His fast "in the power of the Spirit" (Luke 4:14).

## Declaring the Word of God

When you start to declare out loud the words of the Bible with faith and revelation, angels immediately get to work. They respond as if God Himself is speaking because, after all, it *is* God's Word and they recognize it. Angels hearken to the carry out the Word of the Lord (Ps. 103:20). Start daily to speak out loud the Word of God, especially regarding your situation or promise.

## Thoughts

"For as he thinks in his heart, so is he" (Prov. 23:7, NKJV). When you think about the promises of God over your life and destiny, it starts to propel your spirit, mind, and emotions into a higher state of God's glory. The opposite is also true. When you focus on the obstacles, attacks, and impossibilities, it lowers your faith, brings discouragement, and overall lowers your vibrational frequency of God's glory in and through you.

## Faith actions

When you begin to step out in faith, it releases a huge wave of glory. For example, when you are in a store or walking down the street and ask if you could pray for a person that is sick, suddenly a supernatuaral power gets released instantly that was not sensed just minutes before. Once you cross that line and take a step of faith in any area that God is directing you, it attracts angels and God supernatural glory all over your life to carry it out.

## Sacrifical giving

All throughout the Bible when men and women of God give sacrifically it opens a window of heaven. Malachi 3:10 promises God will "open for you the windows of heaven" through giving (NKJV). When Elijah put the sacrifice on the altar, the fire of God came and burned up the sacrifice and brought victory (1 Kings 18:36–40). When King Solomon gave himself and prayed before the altar, the glory of God came into the temple (2 Chron. 7:1). Acts 4 tells us that as believers were gathered, they not only worshiped but gave even the price of homes and land that were sold to contribute to the new move of God (vv. 32–37). That move is recorded from that time onward.

## Blood

When you apply the blood of Jesus to cleanse, protect, and heal, the vibrational frequency affects you even as deep as your

DNA. When you take communion it activates your DNA to the glory of God and releases resurrection power. Blood activates the covenant between God and man. It also supercharges your DNA. That's why many report being healed when taking communion. The blood releases such power that Jesus even said those that would eat His flesh and drink His blood will not die.

> This is the bread which comes down from heaven, that one may eat of it and not die. I am the living bread which came down from heaven. If anyone eats of this bread, he will live forever....Most assuredly, I say to you, unless you eat the flesh of the Son of Man and drink His blood, you have no life in you. Whoever eats My flesh and drinks My blood has eternal life, and I will raise him up at the last day. For My flesh is food indeed, and My blood is drink indeed. He who eats My flesh and drinks My blood abides in Me, and I in him. As the living Father sent Me, and I live because of the Father, so he who feeds on Me will live because of Me.
>
> —JOHN 6:50–51, 53–57, NKJV

# NOTES

## CHAPTER 4
## New DNA

1. Information about John the Apostle found at Voice of the Martyrs' Persecution Blog, "Boiled in Oil but Remains Alive," September 21, 2006, http://www.persecutionblog.com/2006/09/boiled_in_oil_b.html (accessed October 11, 2013).

## CHAPTER 5
## Quantum Glory

1. Brian Greene, *The Elegant Universe* (New York: Vintage Books, 2000).
2. Masaru Emoto, *The Hidden Messages in Water* (Hillsboro, OR: Beyond Words, 2004).
3. Ibid.

## CHAPTER 6
## Sound and Glory

1. Harold J. Chadwick, *How to Be Filled with Spiritual Power* (Orlando, FL: Bridge-Logos, 2006).
2. John G. Lake, *Adventures in God* (Tulsa, OK: Harrison House, 1991), 30.
3. Greene, 146.
4. Emoto.
5. NASA rock sample sound information at www.gsfc.nasa/science-ques2003/20031003.htmheadlinesy20032003/09sep_blackholesounds.htm.
6. NASA sounds from black hole information at http://www.nasa.gov/centers/marshall/news/news/releases/2003/03-152.html.
7. High-intensity focused ultrasound information found at National Cancer Institute, http://www.cancer.gov/cancertopics/pdq/treatment/prostate/Patient/page4#Keypoint24 (accessed October 12, 2013).
8. Kevin Trudeau, *Natural Cures* (Elk Grove Village, IL: Alliance, 2004), 267.

## CHAPTER 7
## Syncing with Heaven

1. Fred Mobley, "Is Easter Biblical," found at http://www.reflecthisglory.org/study/easter.htm (accessed September 12, 2013).

# OTHER BOOKS
# BY THE AUTHOR


*JUMPSTART:*
*21 Days-Natural to Super Natural Health*

*GLORY INVASION:*
*Walking under an Open Heaven*

*MYSTERIES OF THE GLORY UNVEILED*

*ANCIENT PORTALS OF HEAVEN*

*LIVING IN THE GLORY EVERYDAY*

*DESPERATE FOR NEW WINE*

# ABOUT THE AUTHOR

David is the co-founder of DHM and co-hosts a weekly TV program called "The Glory Zone". His passion is to live in the Glory Realm, equip believers to do the greater works and to bring the gospel to as many souls as possible in every nation of the world. David is has also authored 8 books.

David has ministered in evangelistic campaigns, conferences, revivals and outreaches worldwide across every continent in over 50 nations. He has seen revivals break out for weeks up to 6 months at a time. God uses him evangelism and revival services often moving in healings, creative miracles and signs and wonders along with a solid revelatory and teaching mantle to equip believers how to live and operate in the supernatural and glory realm and reach the lost.

David has been in full time ministry for over 21 years and also lived 12 years overseas ministering to the nations of the world. David along with his wife Stephanie and their 3 children are based out of Sedona, Arizona. He is also a graduate of Christ for the Nations Institute in Dallas, Texas.

# CONTACT THE AUTHOR

**WEBSITE:**
www.thegloryzone.org

**EMAIL:** office@thegloryzone.org
**TEL:** 928-282-9030